I MAY BE WRONG, BUT I DOUBT IT:

How Accounting Information Undermines Profitability

I MAY BE WRONG, BUT I DOUBT IT:

How Accounting Information Undermines Profitability

Douglas T. Hicks, CPA, CMC

President

D. T. Hicks & Co.

Library of Congress Cataloging-in-Publication Data:

Hicks, Douglas T., 1948-

    I may be wrong, but I doubt it: how accounting information undermines profitability / Douglas T. Hicks

       p. 116   cm.

       Includes bibliographic references

       ISBN 978-0-557-03159-7

       1. Management Accounting. 2. Cost Management. I. Title

This book is dedicated to the memory of
Gordon D. Nelson (1931-2001)

CONTENTS

Preface

During the past twenty-five years I have often asked myself the question, "Is management accounting an oxymoron?" Are the two terms *management* and *accountant* mutually exclusive? As an active member of the Institute of Management Accountants, my doubts about the legitimacy of the phrase "management accountant" could be considered heresy. But my experience in working with hundreds of businesses, discussing issues with hundreds of accountants, and exchanging thoughts with scores of academics during the past decade and one-half have convinced me that a real-life management accountant is about as rare as a Boston Red Sox fan in New York.

In my personal view, management and administration are not synonyms. I view management as that group of individuals who make the strategic and tactical operating decisions required for a business to optimize its operating profit. Administration, on the other hand, is a group that supports the smooth operation of the business, insures compliance with outside rules and regulations, and enables the business to keep as much of its operating profit as legally possible. Having talented and effective individuals in both parts of the organization is critical if it is to succeed over the long run. Their roles, however, are not the same. Their interests are not the same. And their mindsets are not the same.

A vast majority of an accountant's educational career is spent in learning the fundamentals of bookkeeping, generally-accepted accounting principles (GAAP), auditing rules and techniques, and tax laws and strategies. Most programs do require that students also take one cost/management accounting course, but even that course contains a great deal of material focusing on compliance with GAAP and outside financial reporting. For decades, the focus of accounting academia has been to prepare students for the world of public accounting and increase students' chances of passing the CPA exam. Management accounting is considered a minor factor in the grand scheme of things to the point that many cost and management accounting educators have expressed the belief that their portion of the accounting curriculum is marginalized and that they are somehow viewed as very junior partners in the education of students.

This emphasis translates directly into "the real world." The lens through which accountants in industry view their world is the same lens they were given to look at the world as outside, non-management compliance experts. Their view is superficial and focused on reporting the organization's overall results to outsiders. As a consequence, their "management accounting" techniques are also based on this view – a view that ignores the true internal economics of a business and focus on how the organization's outcomes should be reported to outsiders.

This distorted view of reality causes management to look at its organization's economics through distorted glass and this distorted view can have serious consequences. British-American anthropologist Ashley Montagu once observed that, "The majority of people believe in incredible things which are absolutely false. The majority of people daily act in a manner prejudicial to their general well-being." This statement is as true for business decision makers as it is for Montagu's individuals. From my experience, a majority of decision makers believe in incredible things which are absolutely false and this causes them to daily act in a manner prejudicial to their organization's well-being.

The objective of this book is not to suggest a comprehensive solution to this problem. The past twenty years has seen too many solutions to "the problem" already – none of them taking the problem's overall depth and breadth into account. The advocates of throughput costing, activity-based costing and management, value-stream accounting, resource-based accounting and the like have all found solutions to "their" problem, but not necessarily to "the" problem. They have developed half-truths, not whole truths. As we move forward, we must be mindful of Alfred North Whitehead's warning that "There are no whole truths; all truths are half-truths. It is trying to treat them as whole truths that plays the devil."

Any solution still lies in the distant future. First, accounting must acknowledge that a real problem exists and attempt to understand its true extent. There is too much in accounting that we blindly accept as "the truth" that is only true when we wear narrowly focused set of blinders. This illusion of knowledge blinds us to reality and keeps us "tinkering" on the periphery of the problem instead of attacking its root causes.

What this book hopes to accomplish is to provide the reader with many of the more serious management accounting issues I have encountered during the past quarter century – both technical and behavioral issues – and suggest possible solutions to many of them. It is hoped that by bringing to light many of the questionable "facts" on which accountants have historically based their beliefs and actions, the management accounting community will stop chasing half-truths around the periphery of the problems and set out to identify and solve the real problems before the business community comes to the conclusion that I suggested at the beginning of this preface – that management accounting is an oxymoron.

This book is comprised of a series of essays, most based on the executive letters my firm has prepared for its clients in recent years. Each essay or chapter is designed to stand alone, so there will be some repetition when it is necessary to provide a complete argument within the body the chapter. In instances where the repetition would be too extensive, reference is made to the chapter in which a more comprehensive discussion of the issue has been included.

I have become indebted to many in the preparation of this work. D. T. Hicks & Co.'s "regulars" and its 200+ clients during the past twenty-three years have all made contributions in developing and proving the book's concepts. I am particularly indebted to the late Gordon Nelson, who served as my side-kick, foil, and friend for thirteen years, Dan Popa, long-time Chrysler Corporation financial executive whose encouragement and support have been invaluable for nearly twenty years, and my long-time network of advisors and supporters including Gary Cokins of SAS Institute, Ravi Nayar of UHY Advisors, and Dave Schmitt of BKD, LLP. I will always be indebted to both Jerry D. Pierick and Alex Jackson III, whose guidance and encouragement in the early 1980s led to many of the unconventional views presented in this book as well as William Culp and Richard Czarnecki of the University of Michigan – Dearborn who helped lay the foundation for any success I have been able to attain. Finally, I am indebted to my family: Judi – my bride of thirty-nine years – son Jonathan, and daughters Meredith, Marcella, and Melanie without whose support and understanding none of this would have been possible.

Douglas T. Hicks

Farmington Hills, Michigan
November 30, 2008

I MAY BE WRONG, BUT I DOUBT IT:

How Accounting Information Undermines Profitability

Chapter One:
Stewards and Game Players

Over the years, I have found that the decision makers employed by business owners to manage their organizations fall into two major categories: those who view their organization as if it were a living entity and those who view it as if it were a game.

Those viewing their organization as a living entity act as if they were given stewardship of the organization during a particular period of its life. We'll call these individuals *stewards*. Their objective is to pick up where the previous steward left off and provide the organization with the guidance and nurturing necessary to continue its development until the time comes to transfer its stewardship to another individual.

Those viewing their organization as a game (we will call these individuals *game players*), see their organization as a contest in which they must run up the highest score from the time they begin the game until they are either dismissed or find another game to play. They are not concerned with anything that took place before they began playing the game or anything that takes place after they finish the game. They care only about the score they run up during their tenure.

Perhaps a good analogy is to look at an organization as a team of young baseball prospects and the decision maker as its manager. The steward-manager will take into account the athletes' intellectual, emotional, and physical maturity, visualize the long-term objectives of the team, and manage to a set of interim goals that will keep the team moving toward its long-term objectives. The steward-manager will build on what previous managers have accomplished and do nothing that would jeopardize the success of the team after his or her own tenure as manager has ended.

The game player-manager, on the other hand, will risk the long-term health of the young prospects by pumping them full of steroids to make them stronger and faster during his or her tenure. The game player-manager will teach the young, fragile-elbowed pitchers to break off curves, screwballs, and split fingers despite the risk of permanent damage to their still developing arms. The game player-manager will do everything possible to win as many games as possible by as big a margin as possible until his or her tenure as manager ends. To a game player-manager, neither the condition of the team nor any individual team member at the end of his or her tenure is of any consequence.

For reasons that may be apparent, most of the stewards I've encountered work for family-owned companies. This does not mean that all family-owned businesses are managed by stewards – many of the family-owned businesses I've visited are clearly managed by game players – it simply means that true stewards tend to work for this type of organization where real long-term results are more important than illusory short-term results. Whether family members or hired guns, these decision makers see the organization as a living entity that needs to be guided and nurtured in a way that will allow it to survive and grow over the long-term and generate wealth for the family for generations to come.

Unfortunately, the short-term "managing to the test" (see Chapter Three) perspective of most twenty-first century business organizations puts a much greater premium on the abilities of the game player than on those of the steward. The long-term health of the organization is sacrificed for the illusion of short-term success. The business' decision makers have no intention of being around long enough to suffer the long-term effects of their short-term game playing so they don't care. The investors are planning on finding "suckers" to buy the business at a premium sometime before the chickens come home to roost, so they don't care about the long-term effects either. Both groups view it all as a game.

The accounting profession has been an unintentional co-conspirator in the quest to stamp out stewardship. After all, accountants are the ones who created "the tests" that our game players use to gage their success. They are the ones who have created the rules and regulations that define the incentives used by decision makers to guide their actions. They are also the ones who promote the belief that a one-dimensional, GAAP-based view of the world through a rear view mirror gives decision makers and investors a valid window into an organization's economic future.

In the auto industry, most individuals seem to view domestic manufacturers' eroding market shares as a function of outside influences and those mysterious "legacy costs." No doubt there is some truth in this view. But outside influences are the challenges management is paid "the big bucks" to overcome and "legacy costs" are nothing more than the long-term effects of game players from the past who made themselves look good at the time by bequeathing their problems to posterity. The hole dug by companies during one-half century of playing games instead of acting as stewards may be the most fundamental problem of all.

At the 2006 Lean Accounting Summit I attended a session on the Toyota Lean Economic Model. Although I had heard and read a great deal about Toyota's methods over the years, the one item that I may have known earlier – but whose significance didn't strike me until I attended the Summit – was its focus on managing a slow but steady growth in volume. In a good market, they will raise prices and pass up potential unit sales to keep sales volume on a slow but steady growth track. In a poor market, they will reduce prices and pass up potential short-term profits to attain the targeted sales volume. They sacrifice short-term results to maintain this course of slow but steady growth because the predictability and volume stability it gives their manufacturing facilities enables those facilities to master their processes, improve their quality, and lower their costs. Just as it is healthier for an individual to maintain a weight of 175 pounds than to have their weight fluctuate over time between 150 pounds and 200 pounds, it is easier for an organization to maintain its long-term financial health with slow and steady volume growth than with volumes that fluctuate wildly over time. Perhaps this indicates that Toyota is a model for stewardship while our domestic manufacturers – with their Wall Street-driven, short-term financial pressures and near-term stock price-driven management incentives – are models for game players.

I recently re-read *"My Years With General Motors"* – Alfred Sloan's memoir from a half-century ago. Granted that one must take everything "with a grain of salt" when reading a history that is written by one of its major participants, but Sloan's description of the decision making process during the years after he became General Motor's Chairman reads much more like a group of stewards than like a group of players. They certainly were interested in making a lot of money (which most of them did), but the focus of actions taken by Sloan, C. S. Mott, Harley Earl, Charles F. Kettering, and O. E. Hunt seemed to have been on the growth and nurturing of the organization, not on the score they were to run up during the next two or three reporting periods. They all had long tenures with the company which may have made it seem more like a family-owned business than the publicly-traded company that is was. It was, however, a publicly-owned organization that was able to dominate the auto industry for decades while it was being managed by these stewards.

The impression given by Sloan was confirmed by the attitude held by my grandfather, Harlie Hicks, who served as O. E. Hunt's "troubleshooter" and special projects man at both Packard Motor Car Company and General Motors for over thirty years. Until his dying day he treated General Motors as if it were a living individual – almost a family member – not some game he had the opportunity to play during his long career.

The views and opinions expressed in this book are based on the assumption that the reader is – or would like to be – a steward. I am assuming that the reader would like to make the kinds of decisions that will give his (or her) organization its best chance to thrive and grow for the foreseeable future. I am assuming that the reader wishes to pass an organization on to his successor that has an even brighter future than it had when its stewardship was originally handed to him.

Although this assumption might be somewhat naïve – most organizations are probably managed by individuals "looking out for Number One" and not actually caring about the company, its investors, its creditors, its employees, the part it plays in its community, or the impact it has on our overall economy – I am an optimist. My hope is that a majority of executives actually do consider the companies they manage as more than a fantasy video game with financial prizes being passed out to the winners and no adverse economic consequences to those parties who relied on the integrity and good faith of their organization.

Game players do not need to know or understand the nuances of their business – they just need to know the questions that will be on "the test" and manipulate affairs in a way that will give them a high test score. Stewards need to know "the truth" about every facet of their business including its internal operations, its markets, its customers, its suppliers, and its competitors. To know "the truth," stewards need economic cost information that is of much greater quality than the inadequate and inaccurate half-truths provided by GAAP-based financial accounting. The views and opinions expressed in this book are not intended to provide a full answer to this problem. Instead, the objective of this book's essays is to heighted decision makers' awareness of the problem, give them several ideas that will help them "stop the bleeding" at their organizations, and motivate the accounting profession to stop marginalizing management accounting and treating it as a second-class step-child in the grand scheme of accounting.

Until decision makers stop playing games and managing to the test and begin acting like stewards and managing their organizations as if they actually care about its long-term success we will continue to lose our competitive edge in the world and maintain our momentum down the slippery slope that leads to mediocrity. Without the active participation of the accounting profession – both its educators and its practitioners – it is unlikely that this metamorphosis will occur. If accounting is incapable of changing its emphasis, it may be time, as discussed in Chapter Sixteen, that the responsibility for providing management with the accurate and relevant cost information they need to make sound, fact-based decisions be taken from accounting and put into more capable hands.

Chapter Two:
The Navigator and the Management Accountant

About two centuries ago there was a navigator who served on a ship that regularly sailed through dangerous waters. It was this navigator's job to make sure the captain always knew where the ship had been, where it was, and how to safely and efficiently move the ship from one point to another. In the performance of his duties, the navigator relied on a set of sophisticated instruments. Without the effective functioning of these instruments, it would be impossible for him to chart the safest and most efficient course for the ship to follow.

One day the navigator began to suspect that one of his most important instruments was calibrated incorrectly. If his suspicions turned out to be correct, the navigational information he provided to the captain – information on which the captain based the decisions necessary to safely and efficiently direct the ship – was inaccurate. After several days of reexamining the evidence and rethinking his conclusions, the navigator concluded that something was definitely wrong with the way his instruments were making their measurements.

No one but the navigator had any inkling that there might be anything wrong with the ship's navigation information. He knew, of course, that he should immediately report the problem to the captain. The captain was, however, a strict disciplinarian and was likely to blame him for not detecting the problem sooner. He'd also demand that he either correct the problem or find another way to make the measurements more accurately. Unfortunately, the navigator had little training in the theory of navigation – he had "picked up" his knowledge of navigation on the job while serving on other ships – and was adept at its mechanics, but not the science that lie behind them. He was afraid that this lack of knowledge would make him look foolish to the crew. *As a result, our navigator decided not to inform the captain.*

As a result of his decision, the navigator always made sure he slept near a lifeboat so that if his inaccurate navigational information led to a disaster, his chances of survival would be high. Unfortunately, faulty navigational information caused the ship to hit a reef the captain believed to be many miles away. The ship was lost, the cargo was lost, and many sailors lost their lives. Our navigator – always being in close proximity to the lifeboats – survived the sinking and later became the navigator on another ship.

Two centuries later there was a management accountant who worked for a company in which there were hundreds of stakeholders – from investors who had put their savings at risk in the company to long-time employees who invested many years of their life in the firm. It was the job of this management accountant to make sure the company knew how it had performed, its current financial position, and the likely consequences of decisions being considered by the company's president. In the performance of his duties, the management accountant relied on a cost system that was believed to be a true representation of the company's economics. Without the effective functioning of this cost system, it would be impossible for him to provide the president with the accurate and relevant cost information he needed to make economically sound business decisions.

One day the management accountant began to suspect that the cost system on which he based the decision support information he provided to the president was calibrated incorrectly – it was not based on a valid model of the company's economics. If his suspicions turned out to be correct, the decision costing information he provided to the president – information on which the president based the decisions necessary to direct the company toward its strategic objectives – was inaccurate. After several days of reexamining the evidence and rethinking his conclusions, the management accountant concluded that something was definitely wrong with the way the company's cost system was making its measurements.

No one but the management accountant had any inkling that there might be anything wrong with the company's decision costing information. He knew, of course, that he should immediately report the problem to the president. The president, however, had a no-nonsense management style and was likely to blame him for not detecting the problem sooner. He'd also demand that he either correct the problem or find another way to make the measurements more accurately. Unfortunately, the management accountant had little training in the theory of management accounting – he had taken one combined cost/management accounting course in college but accumulated most of his knowledge of management accounting on the job while serving at other companies – and was adept at its mechanics, but not the science or craft that lie behind them. He was afraid that this lack of knowledge would make him look foolish to the rest of the management team. *As a result, our management accountant decided not to inform the president.*

As a result of his decision, the management accountant made sure he kept his network up-to-date so that if his inaccurate management accounting information led to a disaster, his chances of landing another job would be high. Unfortunately, faulty management accounting information caused the president to make inappropriate pricing, operating, investment, and other decisions that led the company into bankruptcy. The company went out of business, the owners lost their investment, creditors incurred financial losses, and many long-time, hard working employees lost their jobs. The management accountant, however, quickly found a job at another company.

Is This Management Accountant an Exception?

Unfortunately, most companies in operation today are forced to base their decisions on cost information generated by cost systems that do not represent the economic realities of their business. Sadly, a vast majority of management accountants do not plan on doing anything about it. Although supported by twenty-plus years of my personal observations, this statement is not based on those observations. The *2003 Survey of Best Accounting Practices Survey*, conducted by Ernst & Young and the Institute of Management Accountants, revealed that 98% of the top financial executives surveyed believed that the cost information they supplied management to support their decisions was inaccurate. It further revealed that 80% of those financial executives did not plan on doing anything about it.

Personally, I find it hard to believe that the motives of most management accountants are anything like those of the navigator. But if their motivation is not fear of humiliation, embarrassment, or loss of their position, what could be their motivation for continuing to consciously provide their management with inaccurate and misleading information?

It is hard to believe that a 21st Century professional management accountant could be unaware of the shortcomings of cost information generated by systems based on a traditional, over-simplified, financial accounting-oriented model of their organization's economics.

Accountants with many years of management accounting experience cannot have been oblivious to the warnings that have filled professional publications for more than twenty years. Scores of articles have appeared in publications such as *Harvard Business Review, Management Accounting, Strategic Finance, Journal of Cost Management*, and many other accounting-oriented periodicals. Books like *The Rise and Fall of Management Accounting* as well as dozens on topics such as Activity-Based Costing, Lean Accounting, and Resource-Based Costing have sold tens of thousands of copies (my two "niche" books alone have sold over 15,000 copies). Seminars and breakout sessions on the topic have made regular appearances in conferences held by the Institute of Management Accountants, state CPA societies, and other professional and trade groups. Although those receiving the message via these numerous routes may not have believed the solutions espoused by the writers or presenters, the arguments against traditional practices cannot have simply gone in one ear and out the other.

Those management accountants entering the profession more recently have had the benefit of an education that included warnings about old, traditional models and been given the foundation for understanding the options available for creating systems that provide management with the accurate and relevant cost information they need to make sound decisions and take effective actions. During the past few years, I have had the opportunity to review and teach classes based on both undergraduate- and graduate-level management accounting texts, all of which spend a great deal of space on modern costing concepts. These concepts cannot have been totally forgotten by students when entering the workforce.

The impact of *inaccurate* decision costing information on an organization is only exceeded by the impact of *totally misleading* decision costing information. Can it really be possible that management accountants are totally unaware of this impact?

During the past two decades, I have been involved with a number of organizations on the brink of, working themselves through, or newly emerged from bankruptcy. In every case, one of the major contributing factors to their problems was decision costing information that was generated by a cost model that had little or nothing to do with the actual economics of the business. In most cases, the company's cost information was not just inaccurate, it was totally misleading. Their strategies were ill-designed due to misleading economic information. Their pricing policies resulted in increased business that was no where near their "profit zone." They focused process improvements in areas where only "phantom" savings existed. They outsourced or brought in-house products and processes that were better left as they were.

Typical of these was a manufacturing firm that for over five years focused its marketing efforts on a product on which it actually lost between $.90 and $1.10 per unit. Since it sold nearly 1,000,000 of these items annually, the resulting $1,000,000 loss offset the $500,000 profit generated by the balance of their business and slowly eroded its financial position until it filed for Chapter 11. Another company that linked its overhead costs to direct labor focused its process improvement efforts on direct labor reduction while missing the hundreds of thousands of dollars of savings that would have been realized had they understood that the throughput increases available by adding direct labor would have reduced unit costs considerably. Still another company buried the cost of its inefficient fulfillment activities – activities that represented nearly one-third of its operating cost – into its manufacturing overhead rates, making it oblivious to the profit enhancements that were available through improved fulfillment processes and customer behavior management programs. In all of these cases, the development of cost information that represented the actual economics of the organization made the problems – and in many cases their solutions – obvious.

Perhaps it is this failure to understand the financially significant "bottom line" impact of cost information based on invalid cost models that is one of the primary reasons for the continued use of cost systems that generate inaccurate, irrelevant and misleading decision costing information. It is understandable why financial accountants and non-accountants would be oblivious to these problems. However, after twenty years of high-profile warnings, management accountants have no excuse.

There is probably no single answer to the question of why management accountants continue to provide their management with such low-quality decision costing information. My experience in dealing with real-world management accountants (or those who pretend to be management accountants) for the past two decades leads me to believe that some combination of the following reasons has added up to their apathy toward changing their value-subtracting ways:

➤ There actually are management accountants like the navigator. They just don't want anyone to know that they've been providing bad information all along and hope nobody ever notices. Maybe if they ignore the problem it will go away.

➤ Some management accountants just don't have the confidence in their knowledge of the topic to advocate a change to which they know there will be at least some management resistance.

➤ Most top financial executives come from a historical, financial accounting background and still see the primary purpose of their company's cost information as a way to value inventories and measure cost of goods sold. They have little or no appreciation of the impact an invalid cost model has on the quality of their management's decisions.

➤ Accounting departments have so many "got to dos" – made even more time consuming and stressful by the requirements of Sarbanes-Oxley – that they don't believe they have the time for the "need to dos" for their organization to be successful.

➤ The "clutter" of alternative solutions currently existing in the management accounting community makes it difficult for them to determine the best way to solve the problem of inaccurate and irrelevant cost information, so they choose to do nothing.

➤ Management accountants working in a "cost plus" environment where they are required to share their cost information with customers, such as government contractors and in many cases automotive industry suppliers, are afraid that the more accurate and relevant cost information resulting from a valid cost model will result in their customers demanding lower prices.

➤ Many accountants still see the sole purpose of cost information as a way to better determine product costs. They fail to understand the behavioral implications of the way they view their company's costs and the impact it has on their organization's decision making. If they don't see their product costs as being significantly wrong, they do nothing.

➤ At many organizations, management treats their accountants as valuable administrators, but not as part of management. Accountants are agents for compliance, not value-adding members of the management team. As a result, their views on management issues are not taken seriously.

➤ Management has had to work with inaccurate and irrelevant cost information for so long that they have developed coping mechanisms that they believe work and in which they have developed a great deal of confidence – confidence that is usually misplaced.

I'm sure there are many more reasons, but these are enough to highlight the many obstacles that block the path that leads to a company whose navigation system effectively tells its management where it has been, where it is, and where it is headed.

We have often heard people talk of the "captains of industry." It is, however, the "navigators of industry" that provide the captains with the information on which they base the decisions that lead their organization to success or failure. If the majority of these navigators continue to show such apathy toward providing their captains with facts instead of fiction, we can expect many more of our jobs and wealth creating companies to meet their destiny on a deadly reef that could easily have been avoided.

Chapter Three:
Teaching to the Test

For over two decades, those of us promoting 21st Century cost and performance measurement and management concepts have been baffled by the real world's reluctance to adopt practices that not only better reflect the actual economics of their businesses, but also lead them to make better decisions that enhance their organization's performance. Representative of this situation was the 2003 *Accounting Best Practices Survey* conducted by the Institute of Management Accountants and Ernst & Young. The survey reported that 98% of the 2,000 plus participating senior level financial executives believed that the cost information they use to support business decisions was inaccurate. These same respondents also indicated that cost management is a key input to strategic decision making. Ironically, both decision makers and line managers identified accurate and actionable cost information as the #1 priority while, at the same time, 80% indicated that it was unlikely they would do anything to address the problem.

The inadequacy of traditional cost models, especially those based on direct labor, has been widely publicized since the mid-1980s. 21st Century management accountants have no legitimate claim that "nobody told me" when asked why they continue to use such outdated, no longer relevant costing methods. So why do most organizations continue to generate inaccurate and irrelevant cost information – information that leads to dysfunctional decision making – for use by their decision makers?

In Chapter Two I suggested that a management accountant who provided management with decision support information based on a cost model he or she knew to be inappropriate was analogous to a sailing ship's navigator giving the captain critical navigation information based on instruments the navigator knew to be miscalibrated. Both acts seem equally irresponsible – maybe even evil – to me. However, I know many management accountants who fit the description of the navigator who don't seem to me to be particularly irresponsible or evil. So in that chapter, I listed a variety of possible reasons for their failure to address this critical problem.

To this list I can now add another reason – one that I believe may be one of the most significant reasons for the "do nothing" attitude of management accountants in industry. I'll call this reason "teaching to the test."

In the teaching profession, there is an ongoing debate over the value of standardized testing – testing designed to measure the performance of both the student and the educator. One of the more powerful arguments against standardized testing – or at least standardized testing in its current form – does not relate to the testing itself but to one of its unintended consequences. That unintended consequence is "teaching to the test" instead of teaching a core curriculum and critical thinking skills.

"Teaching to the test" means that the test becomes an end in itself. It means teachers focus on the content that will likely be on the test and using the format of the test as a basis for teaching. Since this kind of teaching leads primarily to improved test-taking skills, increases in test scores do not necessarily mean improvement in real academic performance. "Teaching to the test" also narrows the curriculum, forcing teachers and students to concentrate on memorization of isolated facts instead of developing fundamental and higher order abilities. What difference does all this make? Answer this simple question: When you have a serious illness, would you rather have a doctor with an in-depth understanding of his or her medical specialty or one who was good at memorizing isolated facts and taking tests?

In the same way teachers are pressured to "teach to the test," managers of businesses are pressured to "manage to the test" – the test being the upcoming period's GAAP-based financial results. "Managing to the test" means that GAAP-based financial result becomes an end in itself. It means managers focus on the issues that will likely impact the upcoming test and use the format of the test as a basis for measuring performance. Although this kind of managing may lead to good short-term, GAAP-based test results, the improvement in test scores does not necessarily mean improvement in the long-term financial health of the organization. "Managing to the test" narrows managers' focus, forcing them to manipulate near-term events instead of taking actions that will add maximum value to the organization over the long-run.

Not only is managers' performance evaluated against such test results, their compensation is often based on those results. As a consequence, how can you blame decision makers for making decisions that result in good near-term test scores, but lessen the organization's ability to succeed – or even survive – in the future?

This "managing to the test" problem exists at all levels of an organization. Whether it's a plant supervisor who continues to make parts of questionable quality because his "test" is based on direct-labor efficiency or a CEO who defers maintenance, cuts back on research and development and accepts low-margin jobs because her "test" is based on EBITDA (Earnings Before Interest, Taxes, Depreciation and Amortization – see Chapter Fifteen for a more complete discussion on EBITDA), the result is the same; the mid- and long-term underperformance of the organization.

This problem is not new. One of its most common manifestations is "the hockey stick syndrome." This problem occurs when managers "put on a kick" at the end of each reporting period – month, quarter, and/or year – in an attempt to meet the period's performance targets. If measures that will improve performance – such as shipments or direct labor hours earned – are graphed, the graph will look like Figure 3.1 and take on the shape of a hockey stick.

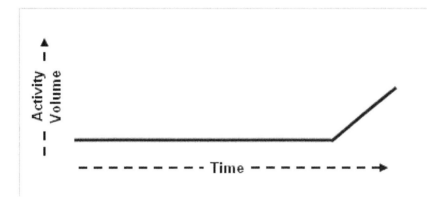

Figure 3.1 – The Hockey Stick Syndrome

I can recall instances of plant managers pulling workers off of their normal assignments to complete jobs that were not due to be shipped for weeks but that were nearing their standard cost "pay points" so that they could absorb more overhead and show greater efficiency during a period. I also recall many instances of shipping ahead of schedule to get sales into a period and then having the customer return the pre-shipped goods – at the shipper's expense – during the next period, keeping the sales book open an extra day or two to increase sales, paying dunnage to hold purchased items outside the plant grounds so they wouldn't show up in inventory, building unneeded stocks of finished goods to absorb overhead, and pulling many other "stunts" that damaged the company's overall results in order to improve the upcoming period's test score.

In all instances, the hockey stick syndrome puts the business' operation out of balance for the beginning of the subsequent period making it necessary to refill the pipeline and balance the operation before moving forward in any kind of efficient manner. The net result is less than optimum performance over the long term in order to sustain *the illusion* of good performance during each individual period. The cumulative performance of the business will always suffer

Another "managing to the test" problem surfaced at a company that created an incentive plan for front-line supervisors that would pay them a bonus of up to 25% based on three performance measures: direct labor efficiency, spending against a flexible budget, and the plant's scrap percentage. For these individuals, managing to the test not only had an impact on the boss' view of their performance, it had a significant impact on their pocket books. It didn't take long for these front-line supervisors to realize that it was next to impossible for them to earn the full 25% bonus every month − balancing these three performance measures was just too difficult. If, however, they generated a lot of scrap − which improved their efficiency and increased their flexible budget − they found they could get an 18% bonus almost every month. To solve their scrap problems they would have to reduce their direct labor efficiency and the level of their flexible budget (which was based on labor hours earned), so they figured they would sacrifice the company's overall performance to optimize their personal bonuses.

When this problem exists among the organization's C-level executives it usually permeates throughout the entire organization. At many of today's companies owned by private-equity firms, EBITDA is the primary measurement by which the company's C-level executives are judged. This measure leads to a myriad of high-level decisions that threaten the organization's long-term viability. It leads to deterioration in the company's capital asset base, failure to develop new products, services, or processes, deferral of critical maintenance, acceptance of marginal orders, and adoption of questionable accounting practices. The lower-level managers working within the organization are then measured by how well they damage the company's long-term success and do everything they can to score high on the upcoming test.

Generally-accepted accounting principles (GAAP) are designed to record the set of non-recurring aberrations that actually took place between two balance sheet dates, not to reveal how the organization actually performed. Consider a company that requires an annual expenditure of $5 million on research and development if it is to develop the new products that will enable it to maintain its existing volume of business into the future. Under pressure to pass its financial test one year it decides to cut research and development to $4 million. This move increases its earnings by $1 million and enables it to pass the test. But did GAAP actually reveal how well the company performed? Does it show that the company put its future in jeopardy? Does it indicate that it has borrowed $1 million from the future in order to pass this year's test and will probably have to spend an additional $1 million plus to catch up in future test periods? Has management actually done something to make the company a more viable business in the future?

Consider another organization that accepts several new long-term programs based on an incremental pricing strategy in order to improve current year profits. The revenues from these programs will cover all of the variable costs required to produce the programs' products and contribute toward − but not fully cover − the fixed cost of resources used in producing the products.

This move will improve the company's GAAP-based profitability in the year the programs begin. But it will also tie up capacity and prevent the company from using that capacity to produce much more profitable products during the remaining years of the programs. Did GAAP actually reveal how well the company performed? Does it show that the company has dedicated valuable capacity to produce marginally profitable – or even unprofitable products – far into the future? Does it highlight how valuable capacity was borrowed from the future in order to pass this year's test? Has management actually done something to make the company a more viable business in the future?

There are a myriad of actions management can take in a given year to help the company's current GAAP-based results pass the upcoming test. In most instances, those actions only make it more difficult for the company to perform well in the future – a future that will be continue to be driven by the desire to pass upcoming tests, not the desire to continuously improve the performance, financial health, and value of the organization. Managing to the test turns decision makers into the "game players" described in Chapter One instead of "stewards" who will do everything the can to insure the long-term success of the organization.

Chapter Four:
The Importance of Models in Decision Making

"The validity of our decisions depends upon our perception and understanding of reality. Good decisions require good models, and the caliber of our decisions reflects the quality and validity of our models"[1]

— Alfred Oxenfeldt

Individuals use models to understand the phenomena around them. The late Dr. Alfred Oxenfeldt, a long-time authority on decision economics, put it this way, "The brain works by constructing an internal version of the outside world. Its conclusions reflect that internal version rather than the actual outside world; *the validity of its conclusions depends largely upon whether these internal representations accurately mirror the outside world*" (italics mine).[2]

Most phenomena encountered by human beings are far too complex for them to completely comprehend. Whether it is the way the economy works, the way diet and behavior effect health, or the way the universe was born and functions, we cannot completely comprehend all of the complexities involved. Yet we must still function in a world where these phenomena exist. To do so we create "models" of those phenomena that incorporate what we perceive to be its most important parts and the relationships between those parts.

John Kenneth Galbraith and Milton Friedman are both considered eminent 20th Century economists. Yet in their work, they championed very different models for managing the national and world economy. During the 1930s, the Roosevelt administration believed in an economic model similar to Galbraith's. As a result, the Roosevelt administration's decisions were based on a Galbraith-like "internal version of the outside world." During the 1980s, the Reagan administration believed in a model more like Friedman's. As a consequence, the Reagan administration's decisions were based on Friedman-like "internal version of the outside world." The laws of economics did not change, the models used to function in a world where those laws operate changed. It was each administration's model of economic phenomena that determined its behavior, not the phenomena themselves.

In today's health conscious society, there are innumerable models to describe the best way to maintain one's health through exercise and diet. Some believe a person should cut back on carbohydrates while others believe that only calories count. Some believe a vegetarian diet is essential for good health while others believe a diet should include generous portions of protein from meat. Some believe that a leisurely stroll around the mall three times a week is more than enough exercise while others believe a strenuous, half-hour workout is needed every day. Some believe that two alcoholic drinks a day will lead to a long life while others believe that total avoidance of alcohol is a must for good health. Despite the fact that there are universal truths about maintaining one's health, each person will act differently because it is an individual's model of these phenomena that determine his or her behavior, not the phenomena themselves.

Controversy has accompanied ideas concerning the origin and functioning of the universe for millennia. Most recently, debates have raged between those who believe the universe was created and is managed by a supreme being and those who believe it began in a singularity known as the "big bang" and unfolds in a way dictated by the laws of physics. An even more ancient controversy relates to the place of our planet in the grand scheme of things. For over a thousand years it was widely believed that Ptolemy had it right - the earth was the center of the universe and everything else revolved around it. Then Copernicus' concept that the sun was the center of the universe held sway for several hundred years. Today, most of us believe that we live on a small planet that orbits an average star, located in the outer reaches of one of billions of galaxies that travel in an ever expanding universe. As far as we know, none of the facts about our universe have changed over the past two thousand years. It is our model of those phenomena that have changed and determined our behavior, not the phenomena themselves.

Understanding that it is not reality that determines our behavior but our models of that reality, we must then examine the second half of Alfred Oxenfeldt's statement that opened this letter, "...the caliber of our decisions reflects the quality and validity of our models."

Imagine the individual whose model believes that three packs of cigarettes, two dozen donuts and a fifth of bourbon each day are essential to good health. Imagine NASA's chances of success if the agency held to Ptolemy's model of the universe. Imagine the success of the medical profession if they still "bled" patients to cure their diseases. Imagine civilization if we still believed that burning witches kept evil spirits from invading our villages, that sacrificing children appeased the gods, or that conducting trials by combat led to a fair and just society. Today we know that such models would not lead to quality decisions, but at various times in the past they were considered valid. The caliber of the decisions made by people who used these models was very low indeed because their models were of poor quality and fundamentally invalid – just ask George Washington about blood-letting (see Chapter Six).

The same phenomena holds true in business. Organizations with good models tend to make better decisions and be more successful that those with low quality, invalid models. There are, of course, well publicized "macro" business models that define the overall structure and strategy of the business such as those adopted by Ford in the 1900s, General Motors in the 1920s, McDonald's in the 1950s, Federal Express in the 1980s, or Dell in the 1990s. These macro models, however, only describe the general structure and outside appearance of the organization. For a time, following these models can enable an organization to flourish without the existence of valid internal "micro" models supporting them. The superiority of the organization's new macro models over its competitor's old business models is sufficient to make the organization successful.

Time passes, however, and the success of a new business model results in competing organizations copying it. It then becomes much more important for decision makers to understand the inner workings of their macro models in much greater detail. They need to understand the internal economics that make the model work. These micro models within the business comprise the engine that makes the macro model work. For decision makers to make the macro model work effectively in a competitive environment, these micro models must be valid and reflect the economic realities of the organization.

One of the most important of the micro models that exist within any organization is its *economic cost model*. Not its cost accounting model – its economic cost model. An economic cost model is the model that describes the cause and effect connections between an organization's products, services, markets and customers, its activities and processes, and the costs it incurs. This is the model that provides the basis for accurately measuring product and service costs, the incremental costs related to specific business decisions, the costs required for performing key business processes, the costs related to specific customers, markets, and product lines, the costs of managing the entire supply chain, as well as the cost of administering the overall business.

Despite the fact that the two have little in common, most organizations use their cost accounting model as their economic cost model. There are a myriad of differences between these two models – too many to go into in a short chapter – but at this point let us consider one simple example.

A manufacturing firm makes the same product in the same quantities for two different customers – each requiring 5,000 units of product weekly. It charges the same price to both customers. The company has a basic cost accounting system where manufacturing overhead costs are assigned to product costs as a percentage of direct labor and all other costs are classified as selling, general and administrative expense and assigned to products as a percentage of total product cost.

Every Monday morning, this company makes a batch of 10,000 units of the common product. 5,000 units are loaded directly onto a truck and shipped to one of the customers. However, the other customer only wants to receive 1,000 units per day. As a result, the other 5,000 units are stored in the shipping area and 1,000 units are shipped on each weekday morning until the stock is exhausted on Monday morning shortly before that week's production replenishes the stock.

According to the company's cost accounting system-based financial records, the profitability of these two customers is identical – an obvious fallacy.

There is a great deal more work performed for the "1,000 units per day" customer than for the "5,000 units per week" customer. To site just some of this additional work, there are six times as many moves required, five times as many shipments processed, and five times as many invoices prepared. In addition, there is dedicated floor space set aside to store the product as well as inventory carrying cost, including a cost of capital, that relate to the 1,000 per day customer only.

The shortcomings of this cost model are not limited to the inaccurate measures of product or customer profitability. The fact that the company's economic cost model does not measure items such as the cost of movement, storing finished goods inventory, picking orders, preparing and loading shipments, or processing invoices means that the probability is very high that managers do not focus on improving these processes. *What gets measured gets done* and failure to measure items such as these leads to their being overlooked when performance improvement initiatives are undertaken.

As additional shortcomings are identified at this manufacturer, the distortions and overlooked costs will compound, showing the company's simple, over generalized cost accounting model to be an even lower-quality and more invalid economic cost model of the business. "Good decisions require good models," and the low caliber of this company's model will surely result in inappropriate decisions and ineffective actions.

Is Your Organization's Economic Cost Model Valid?

Several years ago, we developed a list of twelve characteristics of a cost model that could put a manufacturing organization at risk. Those twelve characteristics were:

> The company has only a single, company-wide overhead rate, or multiple rates applied on only one type of base (direct labor, machine hours, etc.) for assigning indirect costs to products.

> The company has been incorporating new, technologically advanced equipment into its operations without making corresponding changes in the methods it uses to cost its products, customers, services, and processes.

> The company has been adopting new "lean" manufacturing techniques, such as creating lines or cells, without making corresponding changes in the way it costs those processes and assigns those costs to products.

> The company includes the cost of set-ups or changeovers as part of its manufacturing overhead.

> The company has manufacturing operations that do not always require the same number of operators, but still has only one way

(direct labor, machine time, etc.) to assign those operations' costs to products.

➢ The company does not segregate the cost of purchasing, receiving, testing, handling, and storing raw materials and purchased components and attach them to the materials and components but simply buries those costs in manufacturing overhead or general and administrative expenses.

➢ The company outsources certain manufacturing processes without segregating the cost of supporting those processes (multiple handling, transportation, scheduling, material control, purchasing, inventory carrying cost, etc.), nor does it attach those costs to the outsourced processes.

➢ The company has significant in-process material handling and storage costs, yet does not segregate these costs and assign them to products as they are moved and stored.

➢ The company has significant post-manufacturing activities (finished goods storage, order picking, packaging, order fulfillment, delivery) that are not the same for all products, yet it does not segregate these costs and assign them as customer-driven costs.

➢ The primary influences over the company's costing methods are outside reporting requirements – including Generally Accepted Accounting Principles (GAAP).

➢ The company has certain customers, markets, or product lines that require a disproportionate amount of support, yet it does not segregate those costs nor does it assign them to the customers, markets, or product lines that demand those higher levels of support.

➢ In measuring product or customer profitability, the company either ignores general and administrative costs or adds them as a percentage of total cost.

These characteristics were designed for manufacturers, but non-manufacturing organizations should be able to apply many of the characteristics as well.

Conclusion

The lack of valid economic models on which decision makers can rely has been a major obstacle to business success for decades. In 1919, Dexter S. Kimball wrote, "As a part of modern industrial organization the importance of cost accounting can hardly be overestimated. At the same time there is perhaps no part regarding which so little is generally known."[3] As can be seen from the *2003 Best Accounting Practices Survey* – where 98% of the financial executives indicated that the cost information provided to their decision makers was inaccurate – not much has changed during the past nine decades.[4]

Providing management with cost information based on an invalid economic model of the organization can lead them to make inappropriate decisions and take ineffective actions. In today's highly competitive, world-wide marketplace, it does not take too many inappropriate decisions or ineffective actions to undermine an otherwise healthy and successful company.

1   Oxenfeldt, Alfred R., *Cost-Benefit Analysis for Executive Decision Making*, New York, AMACOM, 1979, p. 67.
2   Oxenfeldt, Alfred R., p. 67
3   Kimball, Dexter S., *Cost Finding*, New York, Alexander Hamilton Institute, 1919, p. 1.
4   *2003 Survey of Management Accounting*, Ernst & Young LLP / Institute of Management Accountants, Ernst & Young LLP, 2003.

Chapter Five:
Economic Realities Overlooked by
Traditional Costing Practices

Traditional costing practices ignore many of a company's economic realities. As a result, they provide decision makers with cost information that is both inaccurate and misleading. In Chapter Four, I listed twelve cost model characteristics that could put a manufacturing organization at risk. In this Chapter, I will expand on those economic realities most often overlooked with regard to 1) raw materials and components, 2) outside manufacturing services, 3) set-ups and changeovers, 4) the operation of equipment, 5) in-process movement and storage, 6) finished goods storage and order fulfillment, and 7) customer behavior.

Raw Materials and Components

Varying degrees of effort and investment are required to support different categories of raw materials and purchased components. Consider the different purchasing, receiving, quality, storage, obsolescence, and carrying costs related to these categories:

> - bulk materials vs. packaged materials
> - standard components vs. custom components
> - purchased items vs. consigned items
> - company-managed inventory vs. vendor-managed inventory
> - items invoiced monthly vs. items invoiced individually
> - just-in-time purchases vs. purchases requiring investment in inventory

At most, traditional costing methods establish one "material overhead" category that isolates a portion of the cost related to the acquisition, receipt, handling, and storage of raw materials and purchased components and then simply applies that cost as a percentage of material or component cost. Although this process is better than completely ignoring the linkage of these costs to materials and components, the "peanut butter" application of the costs fails to recognize the substantial differences that can exist among the various categories of materials and components.

During a project for the Department of Defense's Advanced Research Project Agency (ARPA) we studied the cost structure of six small to mid-sized manufacturing firms. In the study we found that between 7% and 12% of the cost of activities performed by these firms related to the acquisition, storage, and handling of raw materials, components, and outside processors. We also found that the relationship between these activity costs and the value of the items being purchased varied widely. For example, at one company, 80% of the activity cost supported only 30% of the dollars purchased while the balance of the activity costs supported 70% of the dollar purchases. At another company, tens of thousands of dollars of support were provided for material that was provided to the company by its vendor. There was no *price* paid for the material itself, but there was a significant amount of *cost* incurred in having the material available for use in manufacturing a product.

One special category of raw materials and components are offshore purchases. Items are usually purchased from offshore vendors due to the exceptionally low unit prices that can be obtained from them. But there is also an exceptionally high level of support activity attributable to offshore purchases, the cost of which is usually overlooked or ignored in a company's quest for lower purchase prices. Chapter Twelve outlines many of the major costing issues connected with offshore purchases and highlights how much of the savings from exceptionally low unit prices can be an illusion.

Without properly matching support costs with items purchased, it is impossible to measure the true "cost" of these items – only the "price" paid for them is known.

Outside Manufacturing Services

Outsourcing manufacturing activities requires a significant amount of oversight and internal support such as: double and triple handling of products, transportation costs, materials management efforts, scheduling problems, quality involvement, inventory losses, payables disputes, and increased work-in-process investments. Traditional costing methods seldom add any of these costs to the direct cost of the outside manufacturing service. Instead, the activity costs required to support process performed by other organizations are treated as manufacturing overhead and included in manufacturing overhead rates. In effect, support costs attributable to processes performed *outside* of the company are assigned to processes performed *inside* the company. The net effect is the under costing of outsourced work and the over costing of work performed in-house.

In the ARPA study mentioned earlier, we found that the cost of activities required to support outside processors added 3% to 15% to the vendor's price at companies that used them frequently and 20% to 50% to the vendor's price at those firms that used them less frequently. Not an insignificant omission from their calculation of product cost.

As was the case with raw materials and components, without properly matching support costs with the outside manufacturing services purchased, it is impossible to measure the true "cost" of these items – only the "price" paid for them is known.

Set-Ups and Changeovers

Many value-adding activities require a substantial set-up or changeover effort between the manufacture of individual products or families of products. Outside of a pure job shop environment, most traditional costing methods – especially standard costing methods – "bury" set-up or changeover costs in manufacturing overhead rates and apply them inappropriately as part of a direct labor- or equipment hour-driven rate. Even in job shop environments, these costs are often treated as overhead. The net effect is to under cost low-volume products and over cost high-volume products, an error that can lead to pricing errors, the attraction of an unprofitable portfolio of contracts, and poor resource utilization.

Even more importantly, the fact that set-up costs lie "buried" in manufacturing overhead places these non-value adding events under the radar. Because what gets measured gets done, the impact of set-ups on the company's capacity utilization, inventory investment and overall efficiency goes unaddressed. At one of our clients – a mid-sized forging operation – measuring the impact of set-ups on the company's operation led to changes that actually increased the cost of set-ups as more set-up work was performed "off line," but provided enough additional capacity that the company was able to avoid the purchase of two additional forging presses during the next two years.

The Operation of Equipment

Many manufacturing costs are driven by the ownership, maintenance, and operation of equipment, not the employment of workers. The fixed costs of ownership, capital, and occupancy, as well as the variable costs of maintenance, perishable tool usage and utility consumption, have nothing to do with workers working. They are "driven" by owning and operating the equipment itself. Yet traditional costing methods frequently tie these costs to the activities of direct labor personnel instead of linking them to the usage of the equipment. The result is the over costing of products where the operator/machine ratio is greater than 1/1 and the under costing of products where the ratio is less than 1/1.

Failure to separate these two factors of production – equipment and workers – also places critical operating information under the radar. At a majority of the manufacturing firms we worked with during the past two decades direct labor costs were tracked in excruciating detail while critical information relating to equipment uptime, downtime and its causes, and capacity utilization was nonexistent. Many of these organizations had invested hundreds of thousands of dollars in equipment they didn't need because they paid an excessive amount of attention to direct labor efficiency and almost none to equipment usage.

In-Process Movement and Storage

A great deal of in-process movement and storage takes place between value-adding manufacturing activities. Unless all manufacturing processes are organized in a continuous flow, there will be both product movement and in-process inventory investment and storage required wherever the flow is interrupted. The cost of these direct, but non-value-adding, activities is almost always "buried" in manufacturing overhead rates. In-process movement and storage also adds to the amount of scheduling and inventory control work required in getting a product "out the door." Failure to isolate these costs not only distorts the final cost of products, but it hides opportunities for applying lean principles that will ultimately lead to lower cost, higher quality products.

At the forging operation mentioned earlier, in-process movement and storage represented 15% of the work performed by the firm's hourly labor force. Once this cost was isolated – it was determined that it cost about $3.50 every time a basket of parts was moved and $3.00 every time one was stored in inventory – management's attention was directed toward reducing this costly, non-value adding activity. The result was a rearrangement of the plant floor to provide for less movement and better "flow" which, in turn, resulted in lower inventories, easier scheduling, reduced cycle times, and a reduction in in-process movement costs of over 60%.

Fulfillment Costs

Most products do not go directly from their last value-adding activity onto a truck for delivery. They are stored temporarily – whether for a few hours or a few months – until fulfillment activities take place. Different total costs can accrue to two otherwise identical products if differences exist in their post-manufacturing activities. A product that is moved quickly from its last operation onto the customer's truck will cost significantly less than one that is stored, picked, consolidated with other products, and delivered via common carrier. Without considering these costs, which are not product costs but customer driven fulfillment costs, customer profitability will not be known and opportunities for applying lean principles and reducing overall company costs will be hidden.

Customer Behavior

Not all customers behave the same – some are "sweethearts" while others are "jerks." Customer behavior can make one customer more costly to serve than another regardless of what products they buy. Whether it is due to ever changing production schedules, cumbersome bureaucratic procedures, low quotation hit-rates, excessive change orders, or myopic oversight, high-maintenance customers take a much higher "bite" out of profit margins that do low- maintenance customers. Failure to properly track these costs makes understanding customer profitability impossible and hides the opportunities for handling the needs of high-maintenance customers in more cost-effective ways.

Summary

Without accurate and relevant cost information, companies must "fly blind" while making critical management decisions. Including a company's economic realities in the way costs are determined will provide managers with the information they need to make decisions that enhance the firm's long-term performance.

Chapter Six:
Excuses, Excuses, and More Excuses

During the past few years I've heard many high-powered, well-paid financial executives make some pretty interesting statements. Among them are:

> ➤ "Activity-Based Costing and direct labor-based overhead application are simply two ways to accomplish the same thing."
> ➤ "ABC is too complicated – we can understand it when overhead is treated as a percentage of direct labor."
> ➤ "We can't afford to dedicate any resources to improving our cost information while our business isn't doing real well."

After giving their comments considerable thought, I've come to the conclusion that they are all *partially* correct. Let's look at each one of them.

Blood-Letting vs. Antibiotics

"Activity-Based Costing and direct-labor based overhead application are simply two ways to accomplish the same thing." This is true in the same sense that blood-letting and antibiotics are simply two equally acceptable ways to cure a sore throat. Just ask George Washington.

George Washington spent most of December 12, 1799 touring his farm on horseback. The weather was continuously changing – going from snow to rain and then to hail – all with a brisk cold wind. When he returned home, his servant suggested that that he change clothes before dinner, but Washington chose to change later "because dinner was getting cold."

Washington woke up the following morning with a sore throat, but he went out to mark some trees that he wanted to cut down. The next morning found him unable to speak. He sent for Rawlins, his farm overseer who had some practice in veterinary medicine. Washington asked Rawlins to "bleed" him. A pint of blood was taken from Washington.

Dr. Craik, Washington's doctor of many years arrived just four hours later and took more of the former president's blood. When the results were unsatisfactory Washington was bled for the third time that morning. Two additional doctors, Gustave Brown and Elisha Dick, were also summoned. When they arrived three hours later Washington's skin was blue. He was having great difficulty breathing and he emitted shrill sound each time he attempted to inhale.

Dr. Brown suggested the standard treatment of the day - more bleeding. So the good doctors bled Washington again. The flow became very slow and thick as they took another full quart of Washington's blood. Washington became weaker and weaker. His breathing finally eased somewhat later in the afternoon when his breathing rate diminished. The first U.S. president died soon thereafter. It was December 14, 1799.

Some attribute Washington's death to a sore throat. Actually, George Washington died from his treatment rather from his illness. Does anyone believe that if Washington had the option he would have forgone a regimen of antibiotics in favor of the blood-letting alternative? Probably those high-powered, well-paid financial executives I spoke with recently believe he would. After all they believe outdated methodologies with absolutely no valid theoretical basis are acceptable alternatives to conceptually sound methodologies that have survived years of intense scrutiny.

My friend Mo Bayou at the University of Michigan – Dearborn School of Management has stated that *"western style management accounting goes around rather that through the manufacturing process."* I've always thought that was a good way of describing the traditional, direct labor-based costing methods still being used at over 80% of the manufacturing firms I encounter today. Whether a plant-wide, direct labor-based rate carries all of a manufacturer's indirect costs or departmental rates are used, these direct labor-based methods avoid having to understand anything about the internal workings of the company – all that needs to be known is a numerator (indirect costs) and a denominator (direct labor hours or dollars) and the problem is solved. Where direct labor goes, indirect costs go in direct proportion. The results are – at least according to these financial executives – just as close to "the truth" as would be the case under activity-based, lean accounting, resource-based, or other more modern costing methods.

Let's see just how equal the two of the alternatives – activity-based concepts and direct labor-driven concepts – are by seeing how direct labor-driven concepts handle some common situations:

- A company has one press that sometimes needs just one operator, but at other times needs two or three. Of course, when two operators are present it costs twice as much as it does when only one is there. When three are required, the cost of running the press triples.
- The company adds some new controls to one of its machine centers. With the new controls it is able to run the machine with only one attendant present instead of the two required with the old controls. It knows the fixed cost of operating the machine will remain the same, so it only considers the variable overhead rate when measuring our savings. As a consequence, it estimates that the variable overhead will be cut in half as the number of operators is cut in half – including 50% reductions in electricity cost, tooling cost, and equipment maintenance costs.

- Every Monday morning the company makes 20,000 units of Product A in a single batch. During the week, 10,000 units are sold to Alpha Co. and 10,000 to Beta Co. at the same price. Obviously, the profit on this product is the same for both customers. It doesn't matter that the 10,000 units sold to Alpha Co. roll right off the end of the manufacturing line and onto a truck that delivers them to Alpha on Monday afternoon while the 10,000 units sold to Beta Co. are first moved into finished goods inventory where 2,000 units are picked and shipped by common carrier each weekday evening.
- The company manufactures two different products that both require the same number of direct labor hours in each of its three costs centers. As a result, the manufacturing cost of each product is identical. It doesn't matter that one product must be moved from a one machine, stored, and then moved to the next machine three times while the other must go through the move-store-move process nine times. Since the total direct labor on each one is the same, the cost must be the same.
- Three of the company's manufacturing work centers – each costing $120 per hour to operate – have just been configured into a manufacturing line. It used to produce 400 units per hour on the first center, 500 units per hour on the second, and 600 units per hour on the third. That made manufacturing costs 74¢ per unit. Now it still has three work centers that each cost $120 per hour to operate but we can only get 400 units per hour through each of them. Since the work centers are now linked together in a continuous flow, they must all run at the throughput rate of the slowest one. As a result, manufacturing costs are now 90¢ per unit. Some improvement, eh?

Do you see a pattern here? Direct labor-based costing methods are *going around rather that through the manufacturing process*. They ignore what actually takes place in manufacturing the company's products.

On the other hand, activity-based models would have separated the cost of workers from the cost of operating equipment. When more than one worker was required to operate the press a multiple of the labor-driven cost (wages, fringes, taxes, human resources, etc.) would have been assigned but the equipment-driven cost would not have changed at all. With separate rates for equipment and labor, only variable labor-driven costs would have been considered as savings when the new controls were added – equipment driven costs such as electricity, tooling, and maintenance would have remained the same. An activity-based model would have identified and measured the additional fulfillment costs for Beta Co. and shown how much lower Beta's profitability is than Alpha's due to the extra services required. An activity-based model would also have identified and measured the cost of in-process movement and storage. It would clearly show the impact that three times the amount of non-value adding in-process movement and storage has on a product's profitability. And finally, since the activity-based model would have measured in-process movement and storage costs, we would have known that movement and storage between the three machines prior to cellularization had cost more than the apparent 16¢ per unit cost increase, resulting in a net savings for the organization and a lower product cost.

You can judge for yourself whether activity-based costing and direct labor-based overhead application are simply two ways to accomplish the same thing. Ask yourself this question; If your company had a sore throat, would you rather put it through a regimen of antibiotics or subject it to blood-letting?

Air Traffic Control

"ABC is too complicated – we can understand overhead as a percentage of direct labor." This is true in the same way that an air traffic controller would think that global positioning is too complicated and want to return to visual control and communication by telephone.

Back in the early days of manned flight – about the time accountants were falling in love with direct labor-based methods of measuring costs – airports were just beginning to realize that they needed to control aircraft traffic between airports as well as near airports. In 1935, the principal airlines using the Chicago, Cleveland, and Newark airports agreed to coordinate the handling of airline traffic between those cities. In December, the first Airway Traffic Control Center opened at Newark, New Jersey. Additional centers at Chicago and Cleveland followed in 1936.

The early en route controllers tracked the position of planes using maps and blackboards and little boat-shaped weights that came to be called "shrimp boats." They had no direct radio link with aircraft but used telephones to stay in touch with airline dispatchers, airway radio operators, and airport traffic controllers. These individuals fed information to the en route controllers and also relayed their instructions to pilots. As traffic levels increased, traffic patterns became more complex, and new technologies became available, air traffic controllers capitalized on these new technologies – from radar in the 1940s to global positioning systems in the 1990s – to keep the skies safe for air travelers (as well as the folks on the ground).

Manufacturing has gone through changes not unlike those in aviation. Where once manufacturers produced high volumes of nearly identical products (any color as long as it's black) using production methods that were highly labor intensive, manufacturing has evolved to the point that product variety and complexity are increasing at a break-neck rate, customers are demanding that more and more non-manufacturing services accompany their products (design, fulfillment, etc.), and automation combined with lean production methods have made direct labor a much less important factor (percentage wise) in the production process.

Of course the finance and accounting folks have convinced management that having a more complex method of costing a more complex business is unnecessary. Had they chosen to be air traffic controllers, they would probably be complaining that the global positioning systems that provide them with the accurate and relevant information they need to maintain the safety of the air lanes are too complex and that they should return to the "shrimp boats" and telephones that were simple and understandable in the 1930s.

Of course activity-based costing methods are more complicated than direct labor-based costing methods – they actually represent what's taking place in a complex manufacturing environment. Accountants can pretend they're making a bunch of Model T's day in and day out because it makes life easier, but the complexity of the method must match the complexity of the business if management is to be provided with the accurate and relevant information they need to keep the company from having a mid-air disaster.

The Leaking Gas Tank

"We can't afford to dedicate any resources to improving our cost information while our business isn't doing real well." This makes sense in the same way failing to fix a slow leak in your gas tank because you're spending too much money on gas makes sense.

The initial consequence of not fixing a slow leak in a gas tank is higher gas consumption. The ultimate consequence might be having the tank – and everything nearby – blow up. The initial consequence of not having cost information that represents a manufacturer's economic realities is a fiction-based decision making process. The ultimate consequence of a fiction-based decision making process might be having the business – and everything connected with it – blow up.

The financial performance of a manufacturing firm is dependent on the quality of the decisions made by its executives and managers and the quality of those decisions depends on the quality of the models being used to support those decisions. A cost model built on assumptions that have no relationship to reality (indirect costs follow direct labor) will inevitably lead to poorer decisions and performance than would one that accurately reflects reality. Once the gas leak is stopped you won't be spending so much money on gas.

Since most manufacturers continue to use the direct labor-based model to measure and manage costs, I guess can agree with the late British-American anthropologist Ashley Montagu who stated, "The majority of people believe in incredible things that are not true. The majority of people daily act in a manor prejudicial to their general well being."

Ever since Robert Kaplan raised the alarm that "yesterday's accounting undermines production" a quarter century ago, all we've gotten from a vast majority of accountants are excuses, excuses, and more excuses. Apparently, accountants simply do not care about the quality of their organization's decisions.

Chapter Seven:
The Blind Men and the Elephant

During January of 2006, I was the after-dinner speaker at the monthly dinner meeting of the IMA's Ann Arbor, Michigan Chapter. After the meeting, I had an opportunity to "bend an elbow" with John Daly, President of Executive Education, Inc., author of *Pricing for Profitability*[1], and a consultant and educator I've know for nearly two decades. During our conversation, John made the observation, "Don't you think these zealots for concepts like time-driven activity-based costing, Grenzplankostenrechnung or GPK (I was impressed, John can actually pronounce the word), throughput costing, resource-based accounting, and lean or value-stream accounting all sound like 'the blind men and the elephant?'"

I hate to admit it (since I didn't think of it first), but John hit on the perfect analogy to describe the early 21st Century dilemma in management accounting. To begin, let's review the fable that John referenced – that of the blind men and the elephant. American poet John Godfrey Saxe (1816-1887) based the following poem on the fable:

The Blind Men and the Elephant

It was six men of Indostan

To learning much inclined,

Who went to see the Elephant,

(Though all of them were blind),

That each by observation

Might satisfy his mind.

The First approached the Elephant,

And happening to fall

Against his broad and sturdy side,

At once began to bawl:

"God bless me! But the Elephant

Is very like a wall!"

The Second, feeling of the tusk,
Cried, "Ho! What have we here
So very round and smooth and sharp?
To me 'tis mighty clear
This wonder of an Elephant
Is very like a spear!"

The Third approached the animal,
And happening to take
The squirming truck within his hands,
Thus boldly up and spake:
"I see," quoth he, "the Elephant
Is very like a snake!"

The Fourth reached out an eager hand,
And felt about the knee.
"What most this wondrous beast is like
Is mighty plain," quoth he:
"'Tis clear enough the Elephant
Is very like a tree!"

The Fifth, who chanced to touch the ear,
Said: "E'en the blindest man
Can tell what this resembles most;
Deny the fact who can
This marvel of an Elephant
Is very like a fan!"

The Sixth no sooner had begun
About the beast to grope,
Than, seizing on the swinging tail
That fell within his scope,
"I see," quoth he, "the Elephant
Is very like a rope!"

And so these men of Indostan

Disputed loud and long,

Each in his own opinion

Exceeding stiff and strong

Though each was partly in the right,

And all were in the wrong!

So oft in theologic wars,

The disputants, I ween,

Rail on in utter ignorance

Of what each other mean,

And prate about an Elephant

Not one of them has seen!

Although in his final stanza, Saxe equates the blind men's situation with debates over theology, he could very well have been describing debates over "costology." Accurate and relevant cost information is a critical factor in almost every management decision or action. If a company's costing methodology is designed around the perception of a single blind man probing only one part of the elephant, that company is destined to fall far short of its value creating potential.

Visualize Figure 7.1 as a diagram of an organization's "cost information elephant." The diagram shows the variety of body parts our blind men can touch as they reach out a hand.

Suppose the first man touches "Process Improvement & Lean Thinking." He will define a cost model that fills his needs. Perhaps it will be a costing model that assigns all costs to a value stream so that management's focus will be on improving throughput and reducing operating costs. He will also try to keep it simple so he can minimize the number of individuals in the cost accounting department. Such a model will work fine when supporting tactical actions related to process improvement and lean thinking, but it will be almost useless when applied to any of the other parts of the elephant.

The second man is concerned with "Inventory Valuation & Cost of Goods Sold." He will define a costing model that takes into account only costs deemed "inventoriable" by GAAP and that accurately measures inventory and cost of goods sold for the organization *as a whole*, but cannot be relied on to measure the cost of any sub-set of the business like individual products, customers, markets, or product lines. This would be a nice simple model – like having overhead rates based on direct labor – but it will also be useless when applied to other parts of the elephant.

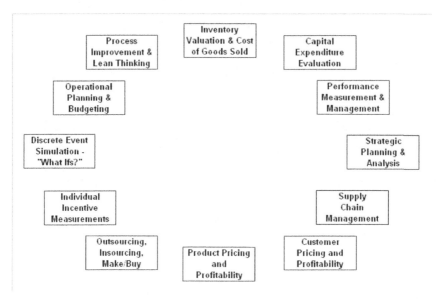

Figure 7.1 – The Cost Information Elephant

A third man is concerned with "Performance Measurement and Management." He might come up with a model like Grenzplankostenrechnung – the giant flexible budget favored by large German enterprises. It will generate great budgets and variances and be useful in controlling geographically dispersed operations from a central point in the organization, but it will require an enormous amount of time and resources to develop and maintain and be of limited use when applied to other parts of the elephant.

Each individual concerned with a specific portion of the cost elephant will define a cost model that fits his specific needs without regard for the needs of others who rely on the output of the model. These individuals will argue with each other incessantly about the appropriate way to design a cost model….

The disputants, I ween,

Rail on in utter ignorance

Of what each other mean,

And prate about an Elephant

Not one of them has seen!

Now I can understand the frustration of a lean organization with the inadequacies of traditional western costing practices in supporting their endeavors. I can understand the desire of financial accountants to apply inventoriable costs for valuing inventory and calculating cost of goods sold in an efficient manner. And I can understand the concerns of managers when their system does not adequately control geographically dispersed operations. But the solution to the problem is not to devise a cost model that looks like their portion of the elephant only. The solution is the development of a valid economic cost model that describes the entire elephant.

A valid economic cost model serves the needs of all interested parties in an organization. Such a model is an accurate representation of the company's internal cost economics. By populating it with the appropriate data – data that will differ from one usage to another – a valid economic cost model will generate the accurate and relevant cost information needed to accurately describe the entire elephant. It will work whether the decision at hand is strategic or tactical. It will work whether the information needed is fully-absorbed or incremental. It will work using historical information or projected information. It will measure process costs, product costs, service costs, and customer costs. As shown in Figure 7.2, it is the engine that takes the relevant data and processes it appropriately to provide support for management decisions and actions of all types.

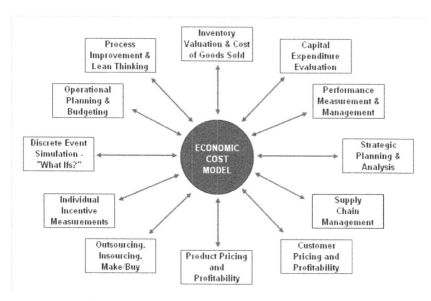

Figure 7.2 – An Economic Cost Model that Represents the Entire Elephant

Constructing a cost model based on only one blind man's perception of an elephant is a terrible waste of a company's resources. It solves only one

53

problem, ignores all the others, and often adds many more. Until management accountants understand that *a valid economic cost model of the entire organization* is the key to providing management with the information it needs to survive and grow in an ever more competitive world, they will continue to "Rail on in utter ignorance of what each other mean, And prate about an Elephant not one of them has seen!"

The solution to the problem is to develop an economic cost model of an organization using activity-based concepts as a "lens" for identifying and organizing the company's activities in such a way that they provide a valid representation of the organization's internal cost economics. Such a model will provide the economic cost information needed by all the blind men that reach out and touch the cost information elephant. Note I did not state that a company should implement or adopt an activity-based costing *system*. An ABC system may be an appropriate means for providing the economic information for some of the blind men, but it is a complex and costly endeavor and should only be attempted by those organizations for which the cost will be worth the benefit, or as my friend Gary Cokins likes to say, "for where the climb is worth the view."

A detailed discussion of how activity-based concepts can be used as a lens for designing an activity-based model that meets the needs of any and all decision makers and managers requiring accurate and relevant cost information in the discharge of their duties is beyond the scope of this book. Such a discussion can, however, be found in my earlier book, *Activity-Based Costing: Making it Work for Small and Mid-Sized Businesses.*[2]

1   Daly, John, L., *Pricing for Profitability: Activity-Based Pricing for Competitive Advantage*, New York, John Wiley & Sons, 2002.

2   Hicks, Douglas T., *Activity-Based Costing: Making it Work for Small and Mid-Sized Businesses*, New Your, John Wiley & Sons, 2002.

Chapter Eight:
Is Accurate Cost Information Only Required
for "Rare Events?"

While researching an unrelated topic on the internet, I came across an article titled "Product Costing as a Rare Event" that Richard Schonberger – of World Class Manufacturing fame – wrote back in 1994.[1]   In the article, Schonberger emphasized that there is a vital role for accurate cost information in managing an organization, but that the decisions requiring such accurate cost information arise infrequently. As a consequence, he suggests that instead of trying to enhance the old day-to-day, monthly, or quarterly cost reporting system with newfound activity-based accuracy, an "as-needed" method of using activity-based costing information would be much more effective.

These statements are consistent with his comments twelve years later during the 2006 Lean Accounting Summit which I reported in a November 2006 Special Edition of D. T. Hicks & Co.'s Executive Letter. In that letter I reported that "Richard Schonberger emphasized that cost data was required for 'infrequent decisions' – his examples included pricing, outsourcing, drop/add – and further he stated that cost information should be the output of 'periodic ABC analyses.'"

At the time of Schonberger's 1994 article, most of the "hype" over Activity-Based Costing was related to its superiority in measuring product costs and in understanding product and customer profitability. Purveyors of software and the consulting services required for implementation expounded on the financial rewards that would accrue to any organization having ABC's accurate product costing data updated constantly and available to use in managing their operations.   As a prime mover behind the Total Quality Management movement, Schonberger took exception to the overhyping of Activity-Based Costing as a tool for managing an organization's day-to-day operations and pointed out that "since competitive product decisions are made infrequently, product cost information should be reported infrequently."   Schonberger added, "In mainstream TQM, however, non-monetary process data are the lifeblood of improvement projects. Associates collect and categorize the data using process flow charts, check sheets, fish-bone charts, Pareto diagrams, process control charts, histograms, and scattergrams (the 'seven basic tools'). In addition, they measure flow distances, videotape machine setups, calculate throughput times and response ratios, monitor rework, and use customer survey data."[2]

As a proponent of using cost data based on activity-based concepts in supporting management decisions, *I agree with Schonberger's basic contention wholeheartedly*! There are many management tools equal to or greater than

Activity-Based Costing when it comes to managing a company in the short- or mid-term – especially in organizations that have made a strong commitment to initiatives such as TQM or Lean Thinking. The one oversight in Schonberger's argument, however, is that product costing is only one of the many areas in which a valid, activity-based cost model of an organization can prove to be invaluable.

Figure 8.1 – which is based on Gary Cokins' insightful "Accounting Taxonomy" diagram[3] – represents a breakdown of accounting into its various components. Our area of concern – management accounting – can be broken into three categories; cost accounting, cost autopsy, and decision support. Cost accounting represents the calculation of cost of goods sold and the valuing of inventories. Cost autopsy, some of which uses data from cost accounting, represents the analysis of what has already taken place in the business in order to track performance. Decision support represents using accounting *and other economic cost information* in order to make decisions that lead to a financially successful future.

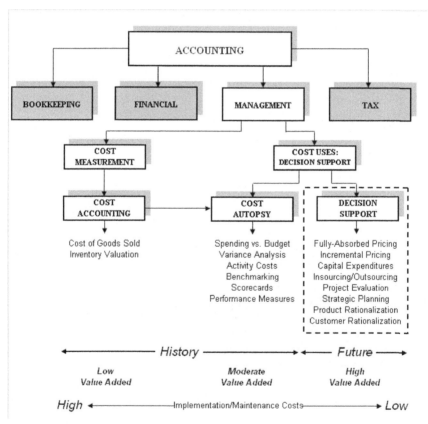

Figure 8.1 – Breakdown of Accounting into its Components

Although it is somewhat useful in measuring past performance, the value of activity-based cost information is in its ability to help management create a more profitable future. Ironically, it is also in its use as a decision support tool that the application of activity-based concepts requires the least amount of time and resources.

Activity-Based Costing's Basic Premise

The premise underlying activity-based concepts is simple; products and services cause activities and activities cause costs. Following this premise, a company should be able to determine what activities are required based on the volume and mix of its products and services. Knowing what activities need to be performed, it should then be able to determine the cost of performing those activities. In Figure 8.2, this is represented on the left or "bottom up" side of the diagram. It is also the way in which activity-based concepts can be used to predict the total cost of running an organization based on the volume and mix of its outputs. Once the total cost of running an organization is known, the process can be reversed. Costs can be assigned to the activities that caused them and the cost of each activity can be assigned to the products or services that made them necessary. This is represented by the right or "top down" side of the diagram in Figure 8.2.

Figure 8.2 – The Fundamental Concept of Activity-Based Costing

Activity-Based Costing is not just about taking historical costs from a general ledger and assigning them along the "top down" path shown in the diagram. It's about having a valid economic model – both intellectual and physical – of an organization that enables management to 1) accurately measure the costs of its products and services *under any volume and mix scenario*, 2) know the cost of its major operating processes (or activities), and 3) accurately measure the total or incremental cost of any proposed business decision or action under consideration. The first two items are accommodated by the "top down" view of ABC while the third is enabled by the "bottom up" view. Its most powerful uses are the first and third although some organizations have found the second one to have the greatest impact on its bottom line.

Product / Service Costing Information

As Schonberger states, there are companies where product cost data is needed infrequently; like when doing product/customer profitability analyses or when setting catalog or list prices. There are, however, many organizations that do not set prices infrequently. Instead, they must quote individual jobs to a wide variety of customers each and every day. They must understand how each item quoted would fit into the company's overall portfolio of business – sometimes on a fully-absorbed basis and at other times on an incremental basis. For such organizations, it is essential that they be able to accurately measure the cost of products – many of which they will never actually produce – every day. This is especially true since one bad pricing decision based on one bad cost estimate could hamstring the company for years to come.[4]

Process Costing Information

Although cost information is not always a prerequisite for identifying and executing operating improvements, it often serves that purpose. At one client, we identified in-process movement as a significant activity and measured the cost of "picking up a basket of parts and putting it down somewhere else" at $3.50. The discovery that "moving parts costs money" and being able to measure that cost set off a chain of actions that resulted in significantly lower inventory levels, shorter lead times, reduced operating costs and improved profits. Had this company been committed to TQM or Lean Manufacturing initiatives, it might have identified and solved this problem without cost information. But the fact is that they had never even given it a thought. In-process movement was just one of those costs buried in their overhead expenses. At another manufacturing client, their activity-based cost model identified and measured the cost of processing orders as well as picking order line items and consolidating parts for shipment – all costs that had been buried in overhead. Once identified, they took actions to improve all of their post-manufacturing process. In the absence of other initiatives, activity-based cost information can often be a prime mover for improving operations.

Total / Incremental Cost Information

Perhaps the most powerful use of an activity-based cost model is in its "bottom up" mode – the calculation of total or incremental costs resulting from a possible course of action. Most management decisions require this type of cost information. The items listed in Figure 8.1 under decision support list some of these decisions. Incremental pricing, capital expenditures, in- and out-sourcing, and product or customer drop/add decisions are just a few examples. The ability to accurately measure the net impact of these types of decisions is critical to the quality of management's decisions. For example, one client had all but decided to close down a line that manufactured one of its primary components because it found a vendor that would sell that component to them at an extremely attractive price. Their costing and pricing manager – who was "the owner" of the company's activity-based cost model – convinced them to "run it through the model" before making a final decision. The fifteen minutes it took to run "before and after" scenarios saved the company from making a mistake that would have cost it $2.5 million annually.

Conclusion

Believing that activity-based costing is all about product costs is like believing that dentistry is all about pulling teeth. Just as "tooth extraction" is just one tool in a dentist's repertoire of solutions to dental problems, "product costing" is only one of many tools in activity-based costing's decision support tool bag. Although it can be an insightful tool for day-to-day operations, it's most powerful uses are in situations where either the long-term sustainable economics of the business or the incremental impact of a proposed major business action are required. Costs based on long-term sustainable economics are needed to support core business pricing, product line, and market decisions. Incremental cost information is needed to support almost every other business decision – from special order pricing to capital expenditure selection to in- and out-sourcing.

Although an activity-based cost model of their organization is not something most companies will use every day, I would not go so far as to say that a company would only need to use the output of such a model "infrequently" or "rarely." Initiatives like TQM and Lean Thinking are designed to continuously improve the day-to-day operations of a business. An activity-based cost model is not. Instead, it is designed to provide management with the accurate and relevant cost information necessary to support critical business decisions – decisions that require an understanding of a proposed action's incremental impact on the organization or its impact on the long-term sustainable economic structure of the business. It is a *rare* company indeed that would *rarely* need such information.

1   Schonberger, Richard J., "Product Costing as a Rare Event," *Target*, November-December 1994, pp.8-16

2   Schonberger, p. 12

3   Cokins, Gary, *Activity-Based Cost Management: An Executive's Guide*, (John Wiley & Sons, New York, 2001) pp. 32-42.

4   I once had a $24 million manufacturing client that made one bad pricing decision based on cost information from a poorly designed cost model. That one decision reduced their bottom line by $1 million annually until it was corrected – once it was discovered – six years later.

Chapter Nine:

Depreciation – The Embodiment of Irrelevance and Deception

"Money already spent is a 'sunk cost,

and it is utterly irrelevant to decision making"

– Shlomo Maital

"Sunk costs are irrelevant" is a principle stated in this quote from Shlomo Maital's book *Executive Economics*[1] and in almost every book on decision science ever written. Despite this well-accepted principle of decision science, accountants – who like us to believe they are insightful navigators who lead their companies through dangerous financial waters – continue to include their company's biggest sunk cost as a major factor in determining its product, service and process costs. That cost is depreciation.

The greatest sunk cost at many organizations is the money invested in its capital assets. Instead of ignoring this sunk cost, however, such companies "pick a life" from the list of allowable asset lives, "pick a method" from the list of acceptable depreciation methods, calculate a depreciation expense, and then treat the result as if it is both an accurate and relevant measure of economic cost.

In reality, *once purchased, the cost of a capital asset is irrelevant.* Up to the point of its purchase – before the cost becomes "sunk" – the cost is not only relevant, but critical. The benefits to be gained from its purchase should be sufficient to provide an adequate return on the funds being invested. Once purchased, however, its cost no longer matters. What does matter is how the asset in which funds have been sunk can best be used to *make money* for the organization.

There are only two ways an asset can make money for a business organization; it can be sold or it can be used. The money generated by selling an asset depends on its *market value* – not its original cost. The money that can be generated by using an asset depends on its *money making capability* – not its original cost. So why do accountants make such elaborate calculations to take this irrelevant original cost and assign it to products and services?

The answer is simple. Contrary to the public relations propaganda you may encounter, accountants are not insightful business navigators carefully charting courses into the future; they are business historians and compliance experts. These well meaning scribes of history – who always keep a sharp lookout in the rear view mirror – want to monitor where the company has been; how good *were* its decisions. Their objective is not to look through the windshield and provide information to insure the quality of future decisions.

Management, however, needs to see where it is going. Only by looking forward can management make sure the company is headed towards a successful future. Managers cannot afford to incorporate irrelevant, sunk costs in their decision making processes. Instead they must look forward to future, relevant costs.

As a company sells its products and services, it must not only generate profits, it must also generate the funds necessary to preserve its *current productive capabilities*. Existing products and services should not be viewed as paying for *past* capital outlays, they must generate the funds for *future* capital outlays. This means that current operations should be generating the funds necessary to make principal payments on debt incurred to purchase capital assets[2] and pay cash for those capital assets that are not financed. In the past, managers assumed that including depreciation expense in product and service cost provided for these future expenditures. But the calculation of depreciation expense has nothing to do with the future – it focuses entirely on past actions! Companies with older assets are probably not accumulating enough capital funds to finance the future. Companies with newer assets may be providing more capital than needed and may be charging prices that put them into an uncompetitive position.

An Extreme Example that Proves the Rule

During the past few years, I've become involved with at least a half-dozen organizations that have either just been created through the acquisition of a number of existing manufacturing facilities or have recently emerged from a Chapter 11 bankruptcy. In every case, financial accounting for the transaction resulted in capital assets that were valued on the balance sheet at far below their actual market or replacement values. In several of the cases, property, plant and equipment ended up being valued at zero ($0.00).

Following generally accepted accounting principles, these organizations took each capital asset's value, selected a depreciation method and life, and began recording depreciation expense just as they would have had every asset been newly purchased. Those with assets having no value on the books recorded no depreciation expense. This depreciation expense (or lack thereof) was then rolled into their costing rates. Those rates, in turn, were used to value inventory, determine cost of goods sold, measure product profitability, and develop rates for use in quoting new business. Although I see no problem in using such costs to value inventory and measure overall cost of goods sold, using them for measuring product profitability is at best misleading and using them for quoting new business could prove to be disastrous.

Consider a company that owns millions of dollars worth of capital assets – assets that comprise its productive capacity and need to be preserved over time – but that records little or no depreciation expense due to acquisition or bankruptcy accounting. As it moves forward measuring the profitability of its products and quoting new business, it will not be taking into account the need to preserve its existing productive capacity. A substantial portion of the profit it records will be illusory.

Figure 9.1 shows the buildup of a target sales price at a company recently emerged from Chapter 11 that records no depreciation expense – and therefore no provision for preserving its existing capital assets – on its books.

Product Costing Example	Company Without Depreciation
Material	$6.000
Labor	$2.000
Cash Overhead @ 130%	$2.600
Depreciation	$0.000
Manufactured Cost	$10.600
General & Administration @ 10%	$1.060
Total Product Cost	$11.660
Profit @ 10% of Sales	$1.296
Target Sales Price	$12.956
Profit % to Sales	10.0%

Figure 9.1 – Target Price Buildup with No Depreciation Included

At a sales price of $12.96, this company believes it will be generating a $1.30 per unit profit. Based on the nature of profit, it should be able to assume that the $1.30 per unit will be available to make the investments required to grow the business and pay dividends to the owners. If it makes that assumption, however, it will be mistaken. Part of that $1.30 per unit will need to be used just to maintain the company's existing capital – to preserve its current capital base.

Let us assume that after a careful analysis of the level of future capital spending necessary to simply "tread water" – maintain its existing productive capacity – the company finds that it would need to add 30% to its current 130% overhead rate – a rate that represents only currently payable indirect expenses. Figure 9.2 shows the implication of adding this 30% provision to maintain productive capacity. Instead of having $1.30 available to make growth oriented investments and pay dividends, only 64¢ will be available. 51% of the profit is an illusion.

Product Costing Example	Company with 30% Cap Factor
Material	$6.000
Labor	$2.000
Cash Overhead @ 130%	$2.600
Capital Preservation Factor @ 30%	$0.600
Manufactured Cost	$11.200
General & Administration @ 10%	$1.120
Total Product Cost	$12.320
Profit @ 10% of Sales	$0.636
Target Sales Price	$12.956
Profit % to Sales	4.9%

Figure 9.2 – Actual Product Profit with 30% Capital Factor

Over time, this company's sale of products will not generate the funds required for it to thrive and grow. It will not be able to maintain its base, grow, and reward its owners. One or more of those objectives will have to be sacrificed to attain the other(s).

Executives at companies finding themselves in this situation are often quite excited at the competitive advantage they believe this gives them. Some even get so carried away that they decide to fill up their plants with products at a slightly lower profit. If management decides to accept an 8% profit margin, they would calculate a target price as shown in Figure 9.3. The actual profit from such a move is not 8%, but only 2.8% as shown in Figure 9.4. Hardly enough profit to allow a firm to thrive and grow for very long.

Product Costing Example	Company Without Depreciation
Material	$6.000
Labor	$2.000
Cash Overhead @ 130%	$2.600
Depreciation	$0.000
Manufactured Cost	$10.600
General & Administration @ 10%	$1.060
Total Product Cost	$11.660
Profit @ 8% of Sales	$1.014
Target Sales Price	$12.674
Profit % to Sales	8.0%

Figure 9.3 – Target Price Buildup with an 8% Profit Margin

Of course, this example is over simplified to make a point. But the fact remains that using depreciation expense as a factor in measuring actual profitability is misleading in the best of circumstances. In cases where capital assets have been written down as part of an acquisition or emergence from bankruptcy it can be one way to assure that the organization will struggle to survive in the long run and perhaps return to bankruptcy.

The Capital Preservation Allowance

One answer is to develop a *Capital Preservation Allowance*. I first proposed this solution in an article titled "A Modest Proposal for Pricing Decisions" that appeared in the March 1993 issue of *Management Accounting*.[3] This allowance is a forward looking view of capital requirements that replaces depreciation in the calculation of product and process cost and enables a company to effectively accumulate the funding required from current products and services to preserve existing productive capabilities.

Product Costing Example	Company with 30% Cap Factor
Material	$6.000
Labor	$2.000
Cash Overhead @ 130%	$2.600
Capital Preservation Factor @ 30%	$0.600
Manufactured Cost	$11.200
General & Administration @ 10%	$1.120
Total Product Cost	$12.320
Profit @ 8% of Sales	$0.354
Target Sales Price	$12.674
Profit % to Sales	2.8%

Figure 9.4 – Actual Product Profit at an Apparent 8% Profit Margin

A company whose capital assets form a single system that is used to produce nearly all of its products or generate its services can develop a single Capital Preservation Allowance (or CPA – not to be confused with accountants bearing that moniker) for all of its future capital requirements. A company with several lines of business, each with different levels of future capital needs, may need several CPAs – one for each line of business. In job shops, where different asset types have different future capital needs, a different CPA may be needed for each unique type of asset. Regardless of the situation, however, the CPA must look to the future, not the past.

The mechanics of a Capital Preservation Allowance are not complex. In principle, it is like establishing a "sinking fund" to provide for future capital outlays. The simplest approach is to forecast necessary capital outlays for a representative number of years. For CPA purposes, capital outlays mean principal payments on existing and future loans used to finance capital purchases, payments made for currently leased assets, and any capital assets purchased for cash – the annual cash requirements to fund preservation of the asset base. For example, one company anticipates the following expenditures to preserve its existing production capabilities over the next five years:

Projected Capital Outlays ($000)

	Year 1	Year 2	Year 3	Year 4	Year 5	Total
Existing Capital Loans	$ 75	$ 75	$ 25			$ 250
Future Capital Loans	$ 25	$ 50	$ 100	$ 125	$ 150	$ 350
Leased Assets	$ 25	$ 25	$ 25			
Purchases for Cash	$ 50	$ 50	$ 50	$ 50	$ 50	$ 250
Total capital outlay	$ 175	$ 200	$ 200	$ 175	$ 200	$ 850
Average annual capital outlays						$ 170

The simplest way to incorporate this $170,000 average annual amount into the company's cost structure is to establish a $170,000 Capital Preservation Allowance and add it to product cost as a percentage of activity costs. The shortcoming of this approach is that, like depreciation expense, it assumes that the need to replace assets is based on chronological time, not usage. This, in turn, allows for a wide fluctuation in rates from year-to-year due to fluctuations in the company's volume of business. Preserving the capital base is a long-term proposition and as such should not be impacted by short-term events. Instead, it should reflect the *long-term sustainable economics* of the business.

A better way would be to tie at least a portion the CPA to the usage of the assets. For example, if the existing group of assets, including those that will replace them, are expected to operate for 85,000 hours during the five-year period, a CPA of $10.00 per machine hour could be established. This would eliminate variations in each year's CPA amount just because of volume swings. Without this long-term view, a year in which machine hours are 15,000 would generate a CPA of $11.33 and a year in which they are 20,000 would generate a CPA of $8.50. Such annual variations do not reflect the true long-term nature of funding capital expenditures.

Since some capital assets become obsolete over time while others wear out through usage, the ideal solution might be to create a time-based Capital Preservation Allowance for those assets that must be replaced due to the passage of time and a usage-based CPA for those that physically wear out. Either way, a Capital Preservation Allowance will provide a more accurate measure of the capital funds that must be generated through the sale of the company's products and services just to maintain the status quo. The CPA is intended to cover the preservation of existing capabilities, not the expansion of those capabilities. Capital expenditures made to support growth are funded by the profits generated by the sale of current products and services; they are not a cost attributable them.

Conclusion

The inclusion of depreciation expense in any cost information developed to support management's decisions or actions is a serious mistake. Depreciation is simply the manipulation of sunk costs and we all know that sunk costs are irrelevant. To simply preserve its existing volume of business, a company must be able to accumulate the funds required to preserve its capital asset base through the sale of the products and services. As a result, it needs to create a forward-looking mechanism that will insure an adequate flow of funds is being provided to preserve that asset base. The Capital Preservation Allowance is one such mechanism.

There are many refinements that can be made to more accurately include a CPA in the cost of products and services. The critical issue is to make sure a company looks to the future, not the past, in determining the capital expenditure costs to include in your company's products and processes.

1   Maital, Sholmo, *Executive Economics: Ten Tools for Business Decision Makers*, (Free Press, New York, 1994), p.
2   This includes principle payments for past capital purchases because they are being "funded" in the future. It's the timing of cash outlays that is the determining factor, not the delivery of the asset.
3   Hicks, Douglas T., "A Modest Proposal for Pricing Decisions," *Management Accounting*, November 1992, pp. 50-53.

Chapter Ten:
When Is An Expense Not An Expense &
A Non-Expense An Expense?

Accountants are conservative by nature. They will always take the most pessimistic view when devising accounting rules. When a business spends money, it must be able to prove, beyond a doubt, that there is a future value in the expenditure to be allowed to treat it as an investment in the company's general ledger. If it cannot be proved, the expenditure is recorded as an expense. This is probably as it should be when creating financial statements for outside parties who do not have management's intimate knowledge of a business, its products, and its markets. Another benefit accrues to businesses that expense as much as possible; it reduces their income and, as a result, their income tax bill. This is another sound reason for expensing as much as possible in the general ledger.

Market Building Investments

This conservative view of expense versus investments does not, however, result in the accurate measures of performance or cost information that lead management to make sound decisions. A simple example of the distortion cause by accounting's conservative definition of investment occurred at one of my clients in the printing industry. For years, the printer's annual sales were in the $20 million range. This level of business was maintained through the efforts of three salespeople. The owner of the business decided that, after years of stagnation, it was time to grow. To begin building volume, he hired three additional salespeople at a cost of $160 thousand annually. Needless to say, business did not jump to $40 million overnight. After one year, business had expanded by 20% to $24 million. When the time came to calculate costing rates for use in quoting new work, the printer's accountant included the cost of all six salespeople in the company's selling, general, and administrative (SG&A) rate. This, of course, raised the SG&A rate considerably, as a 100% increase in selling cost was spread over a volume increase of only 20%.

Was the $160 thousand annual cost of the three additional salespeople actually an expense that should be included in an SG&A rate applied to the printer's $24 million level of business? The three additional salespeople are not all needed to support that volume of business, so why should all of their cost be associated with that business? In reality, despite what the general ledger says, most of the $160 thousand was a market building *investment*. The owner of the company took $160 thousand of the company's profits and *invested* it in doubling the size of the business over a number of years. In concept, this expenditure was no different than purchasing a new press on which a future increase of business could be run. A new press would have been treated as an investment, so why not treat the three salespeople, or at least part of their cost, as an investment?

Accountants will point out that, unlike a new press, the amount paid to these salespeople cannot be recovered, at least in part, by selling the asset. As a result, it would not be appropriate to capitalize the cost and treat it as an asset on the balance sheet. That may be true, but that does not mean these marketing costs have anything to do with the products currently going "out the door" either. The products currently being sold are both *covering the cost* of maintaining the existing volume of business and *generating the profit* necessary to invest in growing the business. Assuming that the new salespeople were expected to double the printer's volume over five years, the business' operating performance was at least $128 thousand better than the profit shown by the general ledger. They reached 20% of the goal in the first year, so 20% of the first year's cost, or $32 thousand, would be a legitimate cost to apply to the $24 million new base of business. The balance of $128 thousand is an investment. It should not be subtracted in determining profit from operations; *it is a use of the profit* from operations.

With a goal of increasing volume by an average of $4 million each year over five years, the printer will be investing $320 thousand: $128 thousand in year one, $96 thousand in year two, $64 thousand in year three, and $32 thousand in year four. In year five, when the business attains the $40 million level, all of the salespeople's costs will properly be considered an expense. In the meantime, "bottom line" performance measurement should not be contaminated by treating these investments as expenses. Most important, the costing rates used to establish pricing policies should not be inflated by including the cost of all three salespeople when quoting new jobs. This artificially inflated rate could, in and of itself, prove an obstacle to attaining the hoped for level of business.

Library and Learning Curve Investments

Another example of an investment treated as an expense occurred at a client that manufactured low-volume, "customized standard" gages for special machine tools. The items produced by this manufacturer were all based on a few standard models. Customization was needed, however, due to the fact that almost every contract they won required that one of their "standard" gages fit into spaces that were different sizes and shapes. As a result, almost every job was like a custom job. This also meant that every time a new contract was won, a new set of prints had to be prepared so manufacturing would know what to produce. Preparation of a set of these prints took up to two weeks.

As a way to reduce print preparation time, make the company more competitive on smaller jobs, and improve profitability on all jobs, the company decided to invest in a computer-aided design (CAD) system. The company estimated that, once the CAD system was up and running, they could complete a set of prints in two to three hours. After the hardware and software were purchased and the engineers trained, they began using the new system. This first time the new system was used to prepare a set of prints, it took *three weeks*. The second set took over two weeks. Approximately one year after the system was installed, the company could complete a set of prints in the projected *two or three hours*.

Two important activities were taking place during the CAD system's first year of operation. First, engineers were moving down "the learning curve" and becoming more expert in the system's use. Second, the company was building a "print library" that made it possible for engineers to locate the prints of a previous job with dimensions close to the one at hand, make the required changes, and quickly generate prints for the new job. Both of these activities had to take place before the system could produce prints in two to three hours.

Were the costs of these two activities expenses that should have been included in the company's "engineering overhead" rate? Were they "direct labor" costs that should have been assigned to the individual jobs? Or were they additional investments required to make the original investment work?

What difference is there between the start-up costs for this CAD system and the internal construction costs for a new manufacturing line? If key components and subsystems for the new line are purchased for $200 thousand and the company spends another $200 thousand having its engineering and maintenance personnel install the line, all $400 thousand would be capitalized. How is this any different from buying a CAD system for $200 thousand and then spending another $200 thousand having engineering learn the required skills and create the print library necessary for the system to perform to its capabilities?

An unconventional view, but one that may closely fit the situation, would be to 1) view the CAD system as a $400 thousand investment that required a $200 thousand down payment with the balance being paid in regularly declining installments over one year and 2) start assigning only two to three hours of print preparation time to each job immediately. All print preparation time in excess of the two- or three-hour target would be considered deferred payments of the original $400 thousand investment. This way the company can improved its competitiveness on small jobs and its overall operating performance immediately – not because of an accounting trick, but because it realized that the cost of making a purchased asset operative is just as much an investment as the cost of the asset itself.

Although accountants might be uncomfortable with this approach, how much more appropriate would it be to charge the cost of making the CAD system operate directly to the jobs on which it is used before it is fully operative, or as part of an artificially inflated "engineering overhead" rate?

These are just two of the types of situations in which expenditures treated as expenses on the books are, in reality, investments. They may not be items that can be capitalized on the books according to GAAP, but neither should they be thoughtlessly assigned to the products being produced during the time the investment is being made.

Expenditures That Are Not Made

There are many situations in which a company postpones certain costs in order to improve earnings for a particular reporting period. Maintenance is deferred, research and development curtailed, or marketing cut back during a particular Earth orbit around the sun. On the continuum of operations, however, these costs must still be incurred if the business is to maintain is existing level of business. If the expenditures are not made, equipment will break down, new products or services will not be developed to replace old ones, or competitors will begin to take away market share. Such costs cannot be overlooked if an organization is to understand its product or service cost or the true cost of its operating processes.

To maintain its current production capability over the continuum of operations, one manufacturer of wheels for agricultural equipment needed to spend $2 million per year for equipment maintenance. The operation's manager, who had decided that this was his last year in that position, made the decision to improve his last year's earnings by deferring as much maintenance as possible. This way, his track record would be improved and his bonus would be higher. As a result, maintenance costs during his last year were only $400 thousand; just enough so that no major equipment would break down and impact current operations.

Did this 80% reduction in maintenance cost actually improve this manufacturer's operations? Should the lower costing rates that result from this reduction in maintenance be used in quoting new business? If general ledger amounts are used to calculate product costs, the answers to these question will appear to be "yes" despite the fact that future maintenance costs will be significantly higher to make up for the negligence of this one year.

There are certain levels of maintenance, research and development, marketing, and other costs that must be maintained over the continuum of operations if the organization is to keep its current volume of business. The pharmaceutical company that does not spend enough on research and development will show improved profits in the short run, its product costs will appear lower and its competitiveness will appear to be improved. Unfortunately, it will be slowly liquidating itself in the process. For a pharmaceutical company, research and development is at least as important as, and probably more important than, capital spending. Similarly, the consumer products company that cuts its marketing costs below necessary levels can improve short-term earnings and make its product costs appear lower. For a consumer products company, marketing expenditures are at least as important as, and probably more important than, capital spending. A consumer products company that cuts marketing costs below the required level will also be liquidating itself.

Establishing the appropriate level of costs such as these requires more effort and a greater understanding of the business than does simply using the general ledger amounts, but they must be established to keep these costs from distorting a company's cost measurements over the continuum of operations.

Cost Cycles That Are Not Annual

Not all cost or business cycles pay attention to the Earth orbiting around the sun. For example, a major piece of equipment at one company must undergo extensive preventive maintenance after every 12,000 hours of operation. During a normal year, the equipment will operate approximately 5,000 hours. As a result, the cost of performing preventive maintenance will appear in the company's general ledger every two or three years. The annual cost to operate this equipment, exclusive of preventive maintenance, is approximately $500 thousand. Every time preventive maintenance procedures are performed, the cost is $60,000. Is the cost to operate this piece of equipment $100 per hour ($500,000 / 5,000 hours) during those years in which preventive maintenance does not takes place and $112 per hour ($560,000 / 5,000 hours) during those years in which it does? Or is the cost better determined by adding a preventive maintenance cost of $5 per hour ($60,000 / 12,000 hours) to a base operating rate of $100 per hour regardless of when the preventive maintenance actually occurs? The later would seem to be the more accurate choice.

The same situation presents itself in other areas, such as the development of new marketing materials or a new advertising campaign. At times, an attempt is made to match the cost with the periods receiving the benefits. Small organizations, however, especially privately held ones, will prefer to record the entire cost in the general ledger as an expense and improve cash flow by taking the tax deduction immediately. Management must be alert for situations in which cost cycles and Earth orbits do not coincide and make the appropriate adjustments before using cost information in any decisions situation.

Similar problems also occur in many organizations whose business includes an occasional product line. An occasional product line is one in which contracts are won on an irregular basis. In some years, there may be no revenue-generating activity at all coming from the product line, whereas in other years, it will provide a significant boost in sales. Although revenues are not generated every year, costs relating to the product line are incurred every year.

One example of this situation occurs in the trade show exhibit industry. Firms in this industry create, construct, and manage trade show exhibits for their customers. They handle a large number of exhibits that might generate from a few thousand to several hundred thousand dollars each in annual revenue. In the day-to-day operation of their business, they must have a great deal of creativity, artistic ability, construction and project management skills, and the ability to manage events at remote locations. The same skills required to be successful working with trade show exhibits year after year are also necessary in a product arena with much less regularity – museum exhibits. A firm might be fortunate to win two or three of these contracts per decade. When a museum contract is won, however, revenues can run into the millions of dollars.

These museum contracts are not won by serendipity or luck. They must be actively and continuously pursued. A successful firm will incur significant marketing and development costs every year, even in those in which no museum-related revenues are generated. For example, a firm with $20 million in annual revenue from trade show exhibits might spend $200 thousand annually in pursuit of museum contracts. These efforts might result in a $6 million to $8 million job every four years. How should the $200 thousand be handled during those years with no museum business? Should it be assigned to the trade show contracts? Should in not be assigned to anything? How about those years in which museum contracts do exist? Should only $200 thousand be assigned to those contracts? Whatever the solution, it should be obvious that the museum exhibit product line pays no attention at all to the Earth orbiting around the sun. In order to properly determine product or product line profitability, adjustments must be made to general ledger expense information before it can be effectively used in decision making.

Summary

The definitions of cost and expense for GAAP-based financial reporting purposes can be very different from the definitions required to support economically sound business decisions. As a result, even well-designed costing methodologies can generate inaccurate and misleading cost information if they simply "crunch" the "actual" cost information recorded in the general ledger. Cost information presented to management for use in supporting decisions needs to be free of "the deadly virus of GAAP" if company managers are to make sound decisions and take effective actions.

Chapter Eleven:
Accumulated Internal Costs

At every organization there are some activity centers that neither support other activity centers nor relate directly to any specific product or service. These types of activity centers are generally those categorized as customer/market support activities, product/product line support activities, and general and administrative activities. Instead of supporting other activity centers or being attributable to specific products or services, these activity centers support subsets of the company's business – a specific product line, a specific market, or a specific customer's business – or the organization as a whole. The nature of these activities makes it difficult to find a theoretically sound basis for assigning their accumulated costs to specific products or services. Despite this difficulty, the cost of supporting a market should be attributed only to the products and services sold in that market, the cost of supporting a product line must be assigned only to products and services that make up that product line, and general and administrative costs must be equitably assigned to all of the organization's products and services.

Consider the situation at one company that manufactures products falling into two product lines; Product Line A and Product Line B. Figure 11.1 summarizes its pertinent operating information.

	Product Line A	Product Line B	Total
Direct material costs	$3,500,000	$6,500,000	$10,000,000
Manufacturing costs	$6,000,000	$3,000,000	$9,000,000
Product line support costs	$500,000	$500,000	$1,000,000
Costs attributable to product lines	$10,000,000	$10,000,000	$20,000,000
General and administrative costs			$3,000,000
Total costs			$23,000,000

Figure 11.1 – Summary of Pertinent Operating Information

Direct materials can easily be attributed to the individual products within each product line using normal material costing practices. Manufacturing costs can also be attributed to individual products within each product line using the appropriate activity-based costing methods. But how can the product line support costs be attributed to individual products within each product line? One answer would be to leave them undistributed and use them only when evaluating the profitability of the entire product line. The same answer could be given for general and administrative costs. Leave them undistributed, but make sure gross margins are sufficient to cover them as well as the desired profit. *There is, however, no such thing as an undistributed cost.* By not assigning the costs, they are, in effect, being assigned on the basis of total accumulated costs.

For example, if our company calculates the total manufactured cost of one of its products and then adds a 33.3% markup to cover product line costs, general and administrative costs, and profit, *it is, in effect, assigning product line and general and administrative costs as a percentage of total manufacturing costs.* They are part of the markup which is a total manufacturing cost-based percentage. There is no such thing as not assigning these costs to products and services.

The next question that then suggests itself is, "Does total manufacturing costs represent a logical way to assign product line and general and administrative costs?" Let us explore that question by looking again at the two product lines that make up the company in Figure 11.1. $10 million of the costs incurred by the company can be assigned to each product line. If it were to add general and administrative costs as a percentage of the total accumulated costs attributable to each product line – the traditional method of assigning these costs to cost objectives – the rate would be 15% ($3 million general and administrative costs / $20 million assignable costs). The company would add the same amount of general and administrative cost to both product lines.

Would this equal assignment be equitable and fairly represent the amount of general and administrative work performed in support of the products classified within each product line. The costs related to Product Line A represent $3.5 million purchased from outside organizations and $6.5 million of work performed by the company's employees. The cost related to Product Line B represent $6.5 million purchased from outside organizations and $3.5 million of work performed by the company's employees. Product Line A required $3 million more work than Product Line B, work that was being supported by its general and administrative activities. Does it seem equitable to assign the same amount of general and administrative cost to each product line when one required the organization to perform nearly twice the work?

Impact on Product Cost

Perhaps we would arrive at a more equitable and representative method of assigning the cost of these types of activity centers to cost objectives if we did not include costs related to outside purchases in the rate's base, but included only the cost of activities performed by the company itself – its "internal costs."

Using "total costs" as a base, the rate for applying both Product Line A's and Product Line B's costs would be 5.3% ($500,000/$9,500,000). The rate for applying general and administrative costs would be 15.0% ($3,000,000/$20,000,000). Using "internal costs" as a base, the rates would be as shown in Figure 11.2.

	Product Line A	Product Line B	Total
Cumulative internal costs for product line base	$6,000,000	$3,000,000	$9,000,000
Product line support costs	$500,000	$500,000	$1,000,000
Cumulative internal costs for general and administration base			$10,000,000
General and administrative costs			$3,000,000
Costing rates	8.3%	16.7%	30.0%

Figure 11.2 – Calculation of Internal Cost-Based Rates

To measure the impact that such a small change in costing methodology can have on product cost, let us compare the cost of two products from each product line using both methods. The results from costing two products from Product Line A and two from Product Line B using "cumulative total costs" as a base are shown in Figure 11.3.

	Product A1	Product A2	Product B1	Product B2
Direct material costs	$3.000	$5.000	$5.500	$4.500
Manufacturing costs	$5.000	$3.000	$2.500	$3.500
Cumulative total costs	$8.000	$8.000	$8.000	$8.000
Product line costs @ 5.3%	$0.424	$0.424	$0.424	$0.424
Cumulative total costs	$8.424	$8.424	$8.424	$8.424
General and administration costs @ 15.0%	$1.264	$1.264	$1.264	$1.264
Total product cost	$9.688	$9.688	$9.688	$9.688

Figure 11.3 – Calculation of Product Costs Using Total Cumulative Cost-Based Rates

Total product costs are identical for all four products. The results from costing the same two products from each product line using "internal costs" as a base are shown in Figure 11.4.

Since Figure 11.3's total manufactured costs for all four products are the same ($8.000) and the product line and general and administrative costing rates are the same, all four products total costs are identical. However, since the makeup of those costs differ (internal vs. external) as do the two product line costing rates when based on "internal costs," the four product costs using internal costs as a base come out quite different.

	Product A1	Product A2	Product B1	Product B2
Direct material costs	$3.000	$5.000	$5.500	$4.500
Manufacturing costs	$5.000	$3.000	$2.500	$3.500
Cumulative internal costs	$5.000	$3.000	$2.500	$3.500
Product line costs @ 8.3%	$0.415	$0.249		
Product line costs @ 16.7%			$0.418	$0.585
Cumulative internal costs	$5.415	$3.249	$2.918	$4.085
General and administration costs @ 30.0%	$1.625	$0.975	$0.875	$1.225
Total product cost	$10.040	$9.224	$9.293	$9.810

Figure 11.4 – Calculation of Product Costs Using Internal Cost-Based Rates

Although not perfect, the use of internal cost as a base seems to generate a much more equitable and representative assignment of both product line and general and administrative costs to the products manufactured by this company.

Drop Shipments & Pass-Throughs

Two areas where the "total cost" vs. "internal cost" methods make a major difference in understanding profitability are drop shipments and pass-throughs. *Drop shipments* are finished products shipped directly from a company's supplier to its customer. *Pass-throughs* are finished products purchased from a supplier, shipped to the company, and then reshipped to the customer with little or no value being added. In both cases, the primary cost related to the sale to the customer is the purchase price of the finished product. The company performs very few activities and, as a result, does very little work related to these sales.

As an example, let's take the case of a company whose G&A rate based on *total cost* is 15% while its rate based on *internal costs* is 30% (one-half of its non-G&A costs are usually purchased materials, components, or products). This company has an opportunity to quote on a job that involves the purchase of $95,000 of finished product from a vendor and having it shipped directly to its customer. The cost related to the procurement of the products, handling the logistics, and processing the paperwork is $5,000. If it uses the 15% of total cost rate it will add $15,000 to cover G&A ([$95,000+$5,000] x 15%) for a total cost of $115,000. It then adds a 10% profit for a total quote of $126,500. If it uses the 30% of internal cost rate, it will add $1,500 to cover G&A ($5,000 x 30%) for a total cost of $101,500. Adding the 10% profit would bring the quote to $111,650.

Do you suppose the company actually incurred $15,000 in administrative activities to support the $5,000 worth of work it performed? Or is the $1,500 a more representative measurement of the administrative cost? Will the job really be unprofitable if it can only charge $111,650 for the drop shipment? Using the 15% of total cost rate it will appear to lose $3,500 at that price when, in reality (if you believe the 30% of internal cost rate more appropriate), it would be turning an $11,150 ($111,650-$101,500) profit. If the company can get the $126,500 price, more power to them. But in a competitive environment, winning a job where no value is added and material marked up 26.5% is not very likely.

A Word of Warning

Although using *internal* costs instead of *total* costs as a base for applying the cost of market, customer, or product line support activities as well as administrative activities is a simple change that can provide important insights into the true economics of an organization, it does presuppose that the cost of all of the other activities have been assigned with a reasonable degree of accuracy. In other words, this is good way to put the frosting on the top of a cake that has been properly baked. If a company's costing methodology inappropriately assigns the other activity costs, these internal cost-based cost assignments will simply follow improperly assigned costs.

In our drop shipment example we indicated that the cost of procurement, logistics, and paperwork was $5,000. Would your cost model be able to assign the cost of procurement, logistics and paperwork to the drop shipment being quoted? If your cost assignment is all direct labor- or equipment time-based, such an assignment would require a special cost study; a cost study that would probably never be performed. The only costs assignable to the business would be the $95,000 purchase cost. Since there is no labor or equipment time involved, there would be no G&A cost since 30% x $0 equals $0. The cake was baked incorrectly so the frosting could not be applied effectively.

Chapter Twelve:
The "Cost" of Offshore Purchases

Do companies really understand the cost of offshore purchases? More companies than ever are purchasing raw materials, components, and other manufacturing services from offshore suppliers. The reason is obvious; the prices charged by these offshore suppliers are considerably less than those charged by domestic suppliers. But are these savings as significant as they seem? Is the *cost* of an item purchased from an offshore vendor sometimes much greater than the *price* paid for the item?

There are, of course, some obvious costs that relate to offshore purchases that are much higher than for domestic purchases. *Inbound freight costs* are probably the most visible. In investigating this question for our clients, however, we have found many other areas where the move to offshore vendors has added significantly to the client's costs.

Purchasing, engineering and quality costs often increase as the additional work required in dealing with distant suppliers in far different times zones with different primary languages leads to an increase in headcount and higher travel and communications costs.

One of our clients moved several million dollars worth of purchases to several suppliers in China. To support this initiative, they hired two individuals to set up a permanent base in China and manage the new suppliers. Their stateside procurement, quality, and engineering personnel began making regular visits to China which occupied enough of their time that several new engineers had to be hired. Top executives made frequent visits to the suppliers as well. All of this cost remained buried in departmental budgets at the corporate office and was never linked to the parts purchased from these offshore suppliers.

Internal handling costs are often impacted by offshore purchases. Items received from offshore vendors have usually been ordered in large quantities well in advance of their required date to allow for transportation problems. In addition, products produced overseas are often "floor loaded" – meaning that they are containerized as produced with boxes of various products mixed in each shipping container. This leads to increased costs for sorting and organizing upon receipt as well as movement to and retrieval from intermediate storage locations.

The client mentioned earlier had four plants using the parts supplied by China-based suppliers. They noted that having four separate destinations for the parts made managing these purchases very cumbersome so they rented a new central warehouse where all parts from China would be received, sorted, repackaged, stored, and distributed to its plants. The warehouse was staffed with a dozen new employees and a new truck was purchased to make plant deliveries on a regular schedule.

The new warehouse was set up as a new cost center on the company's books and the costs carefully accumulated there. No attempt was made to link the cost of the warehouse to the parts purchased from China, the only parts to which its costs related.

Carrying costs are almost always increased by offshore purchases. Additional storage space must be procured for the higher safety stocks resulting from less controllable deliveries and insurance and tax costs increase. Payment terms for these purchases usually require that funds be spent much sooner than they would under the terms of standard domestic purchase arrangements. Even more important is the increased *cost of capital* resulting from these higher inventories. If an organization can earn a 12% return on a capital investment, tying up an additional $1 million in inventory costs that organization $120 thousand – an amount that offsets part of the lower price of the offshore purchase. Since a cost of capital is not included in most companies' cost models, this added cost is never linked to the offshore purchases it supports.

Obsolescence costs are usually overlooked in costing offshore purchases. Since the lead time for ordering from an offshore vendor is generally much longer than from a domestic vendor, the quantities ordered must be based on longer-term forecasts that are less likely to match future realities. Further complicating the matter is the fact that "unexpediting" an offshore order is usually next to impossible. As a result, items are often received that are not currently needed and, in some cases, may never be needed.

Remanufacturing and rework costs are sometimes incurred to "make right" parts that don't quite meet specifications. When a part is needed and the vendor is overseas there is often not enough time to return the items and/or get replacements. In such cases, rework can sometimes save the parts and enable them to meet the immediate need. The client mentioned earlier needed to buy additional equipment and add two hourly employees to take care of the remanufacturing and rework of parts received from their new China-based suppliers.

Most of the companies with whom I have discussed outsourcing decisions never performed an analysis that measured the *"total cost of ownership"* of raw materials, components, or finished goods purchased from offshore suppliers and compared it with the *"total cost of ownership"* from their current domestic suppliers. Outsourcing was either an action demanded by a major customer "if they wanted to keep the business" or was driven internally by offshore suppliers' attractive prices.

Perhaps a vast majority of the decisions to buy materials, components, and finished products from offshore suppliers have been economically sound. But then again, perhaps they have not. Without costing methodologies that effectively link operating costs with their causes – such as linking the costs noted above with offshore purchases – companies will simply never know for sure and continue to operate either in the dark or after looking at themselves in a distorted, fun-house mirror.

Chapter Thirteen:
The Profit % to Sales Fallacy

Profit as a percentage of sales is an almost universal measure of product or customer profitability. When someone says, "We earn a 10% profit on our sale of Product A," it means that for every dollar of Product A sold a ten cent profit is recognized. It is taken for granted that the 10% profit recognized on Product A is superior to an 8% profit on Product B. When a company quotes a new job on which it hopes to earn a profit, it will add up the estimated cost of the product and then add a percentage representing its desired profit. It is taken for granted that a new job with a 10% profit would be preferable to another one with an 8% profit. Unfortunately, profit as a percentage of sales is about as good a tool for measuring product or customer profitability as a thermometer is for determining a wind-chill index. It only provides one-half of information needed to make an accurate measurement of profitability.

The purpose of a for-profit company is not to show the highest profit as a percentage of sales possible. Its purpose is to provide the best possible return on the owner's investment. Calculating profit as a percentage of sales requires two numbers; profit and sales. Calculating return on investment also requires two numbers; profit and investment. It is impossible to determine the contribution of an individual product or customer to the attainment of the company's overall financial objective without attributing both profit and investment to that product or customer.

Even before investigating the lack of investment in the profit as a percentage of sales measure, let's take a look at the measure itself. Consider the company whose product profitability information is outlined in Figure 13.1. The company has two products; Product A and Product B. Both products generate $5 million in sales and the total cost of both products is $4.5 million. As a consequence, the profit as a percentage of sales for both Product A and Product B is 10%.

Is the profitability – and therefore the desirability – of these two products really equal? Twice as much work is required to generate the profit generated by Product A than is required by Product B ($3 million vs. $1.5 million). Since twice as much work is required, it could be inferred that the investment required to produce Product A is also twice as much as required by Product B. If this $10 million in sales represents the company's capacity, it can also be inferred that the company could generate $15 million in sales and $1.5 million in profit if all of its products were like Product B but could only generate $7.5 million in sales and $750 thousand in profit it they were all like Product A. The existing capacity is only capable of generating half of its potential profit with products like Product A. Does this sound like Products A and B are equally as valuable in helping the company reach its financial objectives?

	Product A	Product B	Total
Sales	$5,000,000	$5,000,000	$10,000,000
Costs:			
Material	$1,500,000	$3,000,000	$4,500,000
Activity Costs	$3,000,000	$1,500,000	$4,500,000
Total Costs	$4,500,000	$4,500,000	$9,000,000
Operating Profit	$500,000	$500,000	$1,000,000
Profit % to Sales	10.0%	10.0%	10.0%
Profit % of Activity Costs	16.7%	33.3%	22.2%

Figure 13.1 – Product Profitability Information

As a first step in evaluating an individual product's or customer's value to a company, it might be better to measure profit as a percentage of the product's or customer's *activity costs* – the cost of all the work required to generate the product's or customer's revenue. In Figure 13.1, Product B's profit as a percentage of activity cost is twice that of Product A indicating that it is twice as valuable. Although not a perfect measure, profit as a percentage of activity cost is certainly a much more representative measure of the two product's value to the company than the traditional profit as a percentage of sales measure. Making this simple change alone will improve a company's ability to pick and choose among the business opportunities available in the marketplace.

It should be noted that a key assumption underlying this example is that the activity costs are an accurate measure of the work required. They cannot be based on an invalid cost model of the company nor can they only include those costs GAAP allows for valuing inventory. Post-manufacturing handling, storage and fulfillment costs must be included as must product line maintenance, customer relationship and administrative costs. For purposes of our argument in this article, we will assume that our example companies have measured activity costs accurately.

Let's consider another $10 million company with five products whose results are summarized in Figure 13.2.

	Product A	Product B	Product C	Product D	Product E	Totals
Sales	$2,000,000	$2,000,000	$2,000,000	$2,000,000	$2,000,000	$10,000,000
Costs:						
Material	$400,000	$600,000	$800,000	$1,000,000	$1,200,000	$4,000,000
Activity Costs	$1,400,000	$1,200,000	$1,000,000	$800,000	$600,000	$5,000,000
Total Costs	$1,800,000	$1,800,000	$1,800,000	$1,800,000	$1,800,000	$9,000,000
Operating Profit	$200,000	$200,000	$200,000	$200,000	$200,000	$1,000,000
Profit % to Sales	10.0%	10.0%	10.0%	10.0%	10.0%	10.0%

Figure 13.2 – Traditional Profitability of Five Product Company

Each of the company's five products generates $2 million in sales and $200 thousand in profit. As a consequence, they each show a 10% profit as a percentage of sales.

This company uses equipment valued at $8 million in the operation of its business. It we attribute that investment in proportion to the company's activity costs the $8 million can be assigned to each product as shown in Figure 13.3. Using the investment attributed to each product, we can calculate each product's return on investment – we have incorporated the denominator required to assess each product's contribution to meeting the company's overall financial objective.

	Product A	Product B	Product C	Product D	Product E	Totals
Sales	$2,000,000	$2,000,000	$2,000,000	$2,000,000	$2,000,000	$10,000,000
Costs:						
Material	$400,000	$600,000	$800,000	$1,000,000	$1,200,000	$4,000,000
Activity Costs	$1,400,000	$1,200,000	$1,000,000	$800,000	$600,000	$5,000,000
Total Costs	$1,800,000	$1,800,000	$1,800,000	$1,800,000	$1,800,000	$9,000,000
Operating Profit	$200,000	$200,000	$200,000	$200,000	$200,000	$1,000,000
Investment in Equipment	$8,000,000	$8,000,000	$8,000,000	$8,000,000	$8,000,000	$8,000,000
% Equipment Utilization	28.0%	24.0%	20.0%	16.0%	12.0%	100.0%
Investment Attributed	$2,240,000	$1,920,000	$1,600,000	$1,280,000	$960,000	$8,000,000
Profit % to Sales	10.0%	10.0%	10.0%	10.0%	10.0%	10.0%
R.O.I.	8.9%	10.4%	12.5%	15.6%	20.8%	12.5%
Profit % to Activity Costs	14.3%	16.7%	20.0%	25.0%	33.3%	20.0%

Figure 13.3 – Five Product Company with Investment Attributed to Products

Although this process provides more relevant profitability information, it is not very practical to distribute a company's investment to each product in such a manner. Fortunately, a relatively simple method is available that can easily be worked into an organization's costing methodology that will enable an organization to determine how the return on investment from each product, product line, customer, or market contributes to its financial success.

The first step in the process is to determine the return on assets percentage that will provide the company's owners with their targeted return on investment. This can be done by analyzing the source of the company's investment and arriving at a composite return on assets rate that will provide the desired return to the owners. Figure 13.4 shows such a calculation for a company with net assets of $7 million but whose value to the owners – the cash they could realize if they sold the business – is $4 million.

First the company identifies the capital provided by sources other than the owners. This would include interest-bearing debt and vendor trade credit. The company in Figure 13.4 has $3 million in interest-bearing debt and $1 million in trade credit. The interest-bearing debt has an interest rate of 8.0%. The cost to the company of this portion of its capital is $240 thousand. The trade credit carries no interest. As a result, there is no cost for this portion of the company's capital.

Source of Capital	Amount of Investment	Net Cost of Investment	Cost of Capital
Company Debt	$3,000,000	8.0%	$240,000
Trade Credit	$1,000,000	0.0%	$0
Owners' Equity	$4,000,000	15.0%	$600,000
Totals	$8,000,000	10.5%	$840,000
Company's Net Assets	$7,000,000	12.0%	$840,000

Figure 13.4 – Return on Assets Calculation

The next step is to determine the amount of earnings the company's owners must forgo in order to invest their money the firm. Since the value of the company is $4 million, $4 million is the amount the owners have tied up in the firm – not the amount shown on the balance sheet of its GAAP-based financial statements. In the case of our example company, the balance sheet shows only $3 million as owners' equity, but that amount is irrelevant to our calculation.

Once the amount of the owners' investment is established, the return they forego because their money is tied up in the company must be determined. The usual method is to use the percentage return a reasonably prudent investor would expect in an investment with a similar risk to the risk level attributed to the company. For our purposes, it could also simply be the target return established by the owners themselves. For the company in our example, the owners expect to earn a 15% return on their investment. The 15% target return results in a $600 thousand profit to justify leaving their $4 million invested in the company. This means that the company must earn an operating profit of $840 thousand to pay $240 thousand in interest and have $600 thousand left over for the owners. As shown in Figure 13.4, this represents a 10.5% return on total assets. As also shown in Figure 13.4, if the return were based on the balance sheet's value of only $3 million for owners' equity, the required return would be 12.0%.

Once the return percentage is established, we can proceed to the second step; the assignment of the $8 million in asset value among the company's activity centers. For example, our company has an activity center containing several large machine centers valued at $1 million. These machine centers operate approximately 8,400 hours per year. This means that a fixed annual cost of capital of $105,000 ($1 million x 10.5%) must be earned operating these machine centers if they are to provide the desired 15% return for the company's owners. In other words, there is a $12.50 per machine hour ($105,000 / 8,400 hours) cost that must be covered – just like any other fixed cost – when the machine centers are in use producing a product. If the sales price of the products manufactured in this activity center covers this cost, the 15% return on investment objective has been attained.

The company also has an activity center that accumulates the cost of supporting the raw materials it purchases. Included in this activity center are the costs of purchasing, insuring, receiving, insuring the quality of, paying for, storing, and otherwise supporting its raw materials before they are put into production. Approximately 420,000 pounds of raw material are used annually and an average inventory of $200 thousand is kept on hand. This $200 thousand investment in raw material inventory also carries a $21,000 cost of capital ($200,000 x 10.5%). Each pound of raw material used by the company has a cost of capital of 5¢ ($21,000 / 420,000 pounds) that must also be covered by the sales price of the product in which it is used if a 15% return on investment is to be attained.

As a final example, the company must maintain a finished goods inventory for one of its customers. Its other customers do not require that a finished goods inventory be maintained. The average finished goods inventory kept on hand to support the 5,000 annual unit sales to this one customer is $240 thousand. As can easily be computed, this one customer's product must cover a cost of capital of $25,200 ($240,000 x 10.5%) if the customer's business is to meet the company's return on investment goal. This means an additional $5.04 ($25,200 / 5,000 units) per unit must be incorporated into this customer's sales price to this customer.

If a cost of capital is incorporated into each of the company's activity centers based on the value of assets used in those activity centers, the costing rates used to calculate a the cost of product sold to a particular customer will include the profit necessary to meet the company's 15% return on investment objective. If the sales price equals this cost, the 15% return will be attained. If it exceeds the cost, value would have been added for the owners – their return would have been greater than the expected return. If it does not equal the cost, the return target would not be attained.

If the book value of assets is used instead of actual value – an approach not nearly as effective as using actual value but better than ignoring cost of capital altogether – the 12.0% return on assets shown in Figure 13.4 could be used. The book value of the assets employed would provide return on investment information for each component of the company's business, but only in cases where they do not vary greatly from the assets' actual value.

The example presented here has been kept relatively simple to make the concept clear. Although its actual application may require a little more thought due to the nuances of a particular business, incorporating it into a real world business is only slightly more complex. Adding a cost of capital to a costing methodology that already represents a valid model of the business – such as one designed around activity-based concepts – is an easy step toward improving the quality of a company's portfolio of business.

Knowing the potential return on each investment available would be of critical importance to an individual looking to invest his or her $4 million nest egg. Such an investor wouldn't simply look at each investment vehicle's dollar return without considering how much of the $4 million would be tied up to earn that amount. So why do businesses fail to take into account the amount of investment required to earn the profit generated by a particular product, product line, customer, or market? Is it because accountants are too married to GAAP and GAAP doesn't allow for assigning a cost of capital to products? Is it because they're too lazy? Is it because they don't think it will make a big difference without ever knowing what difference it would actually make? Consider the return on investment differences on the five products with equal profit to sales percentages shown in Figure 13.3. The idea that profit as a percentage of sales is a true measure of a product's or customer's value to a company is a complete fallacy.

Chapter Fourteen:
The Cost/Price Relationship –
Meat & Potatoes vs. Dessert

Accurate and relevant cost information – based on a valid model of the company – is a prerequisite for any organization that hopes to consistently make economically sound, fact-based decisions. One of the most common cost-based decisions made by executives is the pricing decision. Unfortunately, it is also one of the most misunderstood uses of cost information.

One thing should be understood at the outset: **Cost does not determine price. The market determines price. Cost determines whether or not a company wants to sell at the market price**. The day-in, day-out process of estimating costs and then adding a profit to quote new work or establish catalog prices often leaves the impression that there is a link between a company's costs and the price a customer will pay, but *there is no direct link between an individual company's actual cost and the market price.*

Cost is often used by buyers as a rationale for demanding price reductions. Buyers have come up with some of the most creative approaches for distorting product and service cost calculations known to man as a tactic for convincing vendors that their costs are actually lower than they think. But these buyers are not trying to correct a vendor's misguided cost calculations; they are trying to justify their (and, therefore, the market's) demand for lower prices. The market doesn't care what the vendor's costs are; they just want the price to be lower. *There is no direct link between an individual company's actual cost and the market price.*

Although cost has nothing to do with price, it has a great deal to do with pricing decisions. Over time, the prices a company charges for its products and services must cover all of its costs and provide an adequate return for its owners. Not each individual unit of product or service must cover all of its costs, but the total of all its business must cover them if it is to achieve long-term success. It is the accurate assignment of cost to products, contracts, and customers that enables a company to effectively *manage its portfolio of business* in a way that will maximize its performance.

An Investor's Dilemma

Consider the case of an investor with $1,000,000 who must select four of ten possible $250,000 investments in which to place the $1,000,000. As shown in Figure 14.1, all this investor knows about these possible investments is that the total return on the entire group of ten is 15%. Does this investor have a logical, fact-based means of selecting the four best investments? Of course he doesn't.

The accurate and relevant information necessary to make a sound decision is just not there.

Investment	Investment Amount	Percentage Return	Dollar Return
A	$250,000		
B	$250,000		
C	$250,000		
D	$250,000		
E	$250,000		
F	$250,000		
G	$250,000		
H	$250,000		
I	$250,000		
J	$250,000		
Totals	$2,500,000	15.0%	$375,000

Figure 14.1 – Investor Faced with Inadequate Data

Since no logical, fact-based method of evaluating the investment alternatives is available, our investor must use "gut feel," intuition, or some other basis for a decision. In this case, the investor uses the first letter of each of his four children's names to select the investment vehicles: Albert, Charles, and the twins – Eugene and Imogene. The resulting portfolio is shown in Figure 14.2. Obviously, the 4.5% return does not represent a very successful selection of investments from a group whose average return is 15%.

What if, on the other hand, our investor had the information in Figure 14.3 available when making his or her investment decision? Would the investor now have some facts on which to select the four investments for his portfolio? Of course he would. As shown in Figure 14.4, by selecting Investments B, D, F, and H our investor could earn a return of $242,500 or 24.3%. By knowing the contribution of each investment in his portfolio, this investor is able to maximize his portfolio's performance.

Investment	Investment Amount	Percentage Return	Dollar Return
A	$250,000	-4.0%	($10,000)
B	$0	0.0%	$0
C	$250,000	12.0%	$30,000
D	$0	0.0%	$0
E	$250,000	4.0%	$10,000
F	$0	0.0%	$0
G	$0	0.0%	$0
H	$0	0.0%	$0
I	$250,000	6.0%	$15,000
J	$0	0.0%	$0
Totals	$1,000,000	4.5%	$45,000

Figure 14.2 – Portfolio Based on Inadequate Information

Investment	Investment Amount	Percentage Return	Dollar Return
A	$250,000	-4.0%	($10,000)
B	$250,000	30.0%	$75,000
C	$250,000	12.0%	$30,000
D	$250,000	23.0%	$57,500
E	$250,000	4.0%	$10,000
F	$250,000	20.0%	$50,000
G	$250,000	16.0%	$40,000
H	$250,000	24.0%	$60,000
I	$250,000	6.0%	$15,000
J	$250,000	19.0%	$47,500
Totals	$2,500,000	15.0%	$375,000

Figure 14.3 – Investor Provided with Adequate Data

Investment	Investment Amount	Percentage Return	Dollar Return
A	$0	0.0%	$0
B	$250,000	30.0%	$75,000
C	$0	0.0%	$0
D	$250,000	23.0%	$57,500
E	$0	0.0%	$0
F	$250,000	20.0%	$50,000
G	$0	0.0%	$0
H	$250,000	24.0%	$60,000
I	$0	0.0%	$0
J	$0	0.0%	$0
Totals	$1,000,000	24.3%	$242,500

Figure 14.4 – Portfolio Based on Adequate Information

A Decision Maker's Dilemma

Consider now the case of a company with the capacity to handle $1,000,000 of business. There are currently ten $250,000 contracts out for bid. Which four contracts does the company want?

If the company has a method of accurately measuring the cost and profit potential of each contract, just as our investor knew the potential return of each investment in Figure 14.3, its decision makers will have sound, fact-based information with which to pursue the four contracts that would contribute most to the company's portfolio of business. If, on the other hand, its costing methods do not accurately measure each potential contract's cost, decision makers will be "flying blind," just as our investor was in Figure 14.1, and might pursue the wrong four contracts, resulting in less than optimum performance.

There is a law of economics – known at my firm as *Hicks' First Law of Pricing* – that applies here. That law goes like this: *"A company will get a lot of business when it does not charge its customers for things it does for them, but it will not get much business when it attempts to charge its customers for things that it doesn't do for them."*

For example, one company has overall productivity that is about average for its industry and marketplace. Under normal economic conditions, the market will allow this company, whose costs are at the industry average, to charge a price that will enable it to recapture its cost and earn enough of a profit to ensure its continuing ability to supply the marketplace. If this company accurately calculates its "fully-absorbed"[1] costs and adds a market-supportable profit margin on each of one hundred possible contracts, it should be competitive on those contracts and will earn its expected profit margin on any contract it is awarded.

This situation is shown graphically in Figure 14.5 in which the horizontal axis represents one hundred contracts bid and the vertical axis the percentage accuracy of its fully-absorbed cost estimates. The market prices shown provide consistent margins above the accurately determined costs. The area between the market price and the 100% accurate contract costs represents the profit on any contract awarded at the market price.

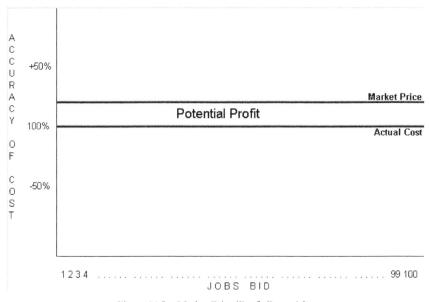

Figure 14.5 – Market Price/Profit Potential

If this company uses an inappropriate, over-generalized methodology (such as applying overhead costs on the basis of direct labor hours/dollars, machine hours, etc.) to estimate its costs, it will overestimate the fully-absorbed cost on approximately one half of the contracts bid and underestimate the costs on the other half. As a result, it will establish an *acceptable price* (quoted price) at levels that will be under the market for those contracts whose costs were underestimated and over the market for those contracts whose cost were overestimated. This situation can be seen graphically in Figure 14.6 in which contracts are sequenced from left to right starting with the contract whose cost was most underestimated and ending with the contract whose cost was most overestimated.

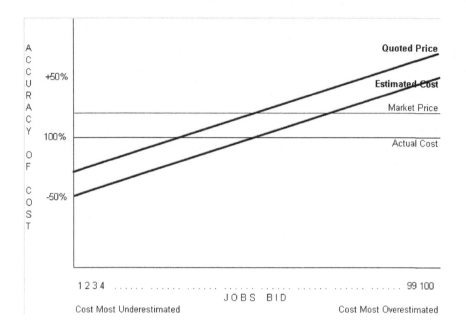

Figure14. 6 – Pricing Based on Over-Generalized Costs

Looking at the "Quoted Price" and "Market Price" lines, it is obvious that the company will be much more likely to be awarded contracts on the left side of the diagram – contracts bid at less than market price – for which it was *"not charging the customer for things it does for them."* Conversely, it will not be awarded contracts on the right side of the diagram – contracts that could have been profitable at much lower prices – for which it was *"charging the customer for things it does not do for them."* Unfortunately, actual costs do not care whether they have been over or underestimated; they will be *actual* either way. As Figure 14.7 clearly shows, if the company is awarded those contracts that were inadvertently priced below market, it has little or no change of financial success. At the same time it will be missing out on the potential profits that could have been earned at the market price on those contracts its inaccurate costing methodologies caused it to overprice.

Pricing the "Meat and Potatoes"

The better-informed pricing decisions and more profitable portfolio of contracts that result from using cost information based on a valid economic model of the organization can have a significant "bottom line" impact. In Chapter 14 of my 2002 book *Activity-Based Costing: Making it Work for Small and Mid-Sized Companies*[2], a detailed example is used to develop decision costing information for a small (less than $3 million sales) company with ten contracts. According to the company's traditional cost information (manufacturing overhead as a percentage of direct labor and general and administrative expenses as a percentage to total cost) its $125,000 profit margin was generated by ten contracts with identical 4.7% profit margins.

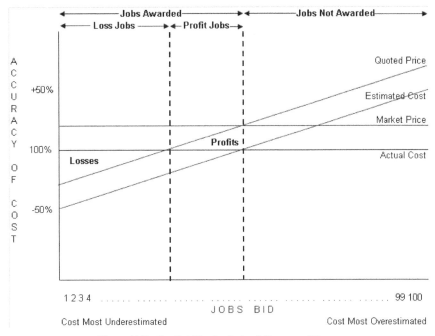

Figure 14.7 – Profitability Analysis of Contracts Won

An activity-based decision-costing model, however, showed that this $125,000 profit was actually generated by contacts with margins ranging from +18.6% to –16.8%. Using the model for further decision-costing analysis showed that if a contract with a 9.5% margin (similar to the company's fourth most profitable contract – one on which it accurately calculated its cost and added a market-supportable margin) had been won instead of its worst contract (the minus 16.8% margin contract – one on which it had underestimated its costs and *did not charge its customer for things it does for them*), its profit would have been $182,000, a 45% increase. Its profit percentage to sales would have been 6.6% instead of 4.7% – an increase of almost two percentage points – if it had simply avoided *one* easily avoidable pricing mistake. Think of the impact of its avoiding *all* such pricing mistakes.

The accurate assignment of fully-absorbed cost to products, contracts, and customers enable a company to effectively manage its portfolio of *core business* – the products or services it normally sells when sold under normal market conditions. Core business is the key to the organization's long-term survival. Over time its sales must cover the bulk of the company's costs and generate the majority of its profit. It is the "meat and potatoes" that must nourish and fortify the organization. However, in addition to "meat and potatoes," many companies also have opportunities for a little "dessert" – incremental business that can prove to be very profitable, but that does not follow the same costing rules as core business.

Pricing the "Dessert"

Products and services that can be classified as a company's "dessert" are its *non-core business*. Not surprisingly (based on my definition of core business), non-core business can be defined as the types of products or services a company does not normally sell <u>or</u> any products or services that are not sold under normal market conditions; simply, anything that is not core business. This type of business is often known as "peripheral" business or "business on the edge."

Just as a valid cost model is required to effectively manage that portion of a company's portfolio represented by core business; it is also required to manage the addition of non-core business to that portfolio. However, instead of using the model to establish the fully-absorbed cost of the product or service, non-core business requires the model to determine the "incremental" cost of the product or service – the additional out-of-pocket costs that will result from adding the non-core business to the company's portfolio.

Organizations with traditional cost systems often attempt to calculate these incremental costs by separating their labor- or machine-based rates into two categories: a fixed rate and a variable rate. They then multiply the incremental labor or machine resources required to support the business by the variable rate to determine the incremental cost of that business. There are two problems with this approach:

- labor dollars, labor hours, or machine hours are seldom accurate measures for what actually drives the other costs of an organization and
- the definitions of "fixed" and "variable" cannot be considered constant, they are *situation specific*.

This results in inaccurate and misleading cost information being presented to decision makers as they determine the advisability of adding non-core business to the company's portfolio. On the other hand, a valid cost model of the organization accommodates the semi-fixed and step-variable costs that are critical to all "incremental" cost-based decisions and, because it is based on actual cause-and-effect relationships, effectively measures the impact on variable costs of the business under consideration.

Beware of Too Much Dessert

There are many legitimate uses of "dessert pricing" that help a company better use its capacity and improve its financial performance. One-time special orders are a good example. Selling seasonal or normal excess capacity in a secondary market is another. But many organizations have gotten themselves into deep trouble by failing to control their appetite for dessert.

In their desire to increase sales, these organizations use incremental cost information as a basis for rationalizing prices that do not cover the fully-absorbed cost of core business. Although this strategy may work in the short-term to fill otherwise unused capacity, its long-term use can be fatal – just as an occasional dessert "binge" at a holiday party won't cause immediate cardiac arrest, but a diet consisting primarily of desserts will lead to an early grave. Treating core business as "business on the edges" shrinks the amount of a company's capacity left to cover the fundamental costs required to remain in business over the long-term. A company whose mix of core and peripheral business can be represented by the diagram on the left in Figure 14.8 has a much greater chance of success than one whose mix is better expressed in the diagram on the right.

Conclusion

Accurate knowledge of product and service cost is critical for any organization that hopes to thrive and grow in a competitive business environment. The vast majority of business in a company's portfolio – its core business – must be sold at prices that cover its fully-absorbed cost. Profits can be further enhanced by the judicious use of incremental costs in determining acceptable prices for "business on the edges." But expanding the use of incremental cost into the evaluation of core business is a formula for disaster.

Without the ability to accurately measure the cost of its products or services, whether the appropriate costs are fully-absorbed or incremental, a company will not be able to manage its portfolio of business in a way that maximizes its financial performance and adds value for its stakeholders. Traditional costing methods, those based on labor hours, labor dollars, or machine hours, seldom provide the levels of accuracy needed by decision makers. Only a well-designed, activity-based model of the organization can provide the insights necessary.[3]

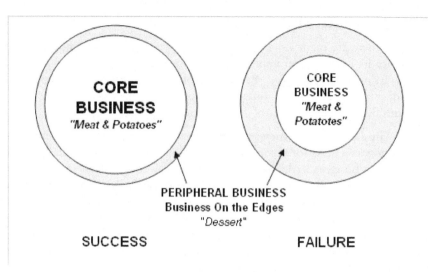

Figure 14.8 – Blending Core and Peripheral Business

1   "Fully-absorbed" costs are product or service costs where each product or services picks up its "fair share" – based on cause-and-effect relationships – of all of the costs incurred by the organization, both fixed and variable.

2   Hicks, Douglas T., *Activity-Based Costing: Making it Work for Small and Mid-Sized Companies*, (New York, John Wiley & Sons, 2002)

3   Specific applications of these principles for special order pricing, strategic pricing, product line pricing, and long-term contracts are covered in more detail on pages 110-128 of *Activity-Based Costing: Making it Work for Small and Mid-Sized Companies* (see footnote 2).

Chapter Fifteen:
Eschewing EBITDA

It seems that more and more of the companies that drive our economy and employ our citizens are being purchased by private-equity firms and investment banks. Here in the Midwest, it seems like a private-equity firm is taking over a key player in the automotive industry every time one picks up the business news. The ultimate financial gain for these firms comes when they eventually divest of the acquired company – hopefully at a substantial profit.

EBITDA – Earnings Before Interest, Taxes, Depreciation, and Amortization – appears to have become the most popular corporate performance measurement for investors such as these. It appeals to them because it gives them a measure of how much a steeply leveraged buyer can afford to pay for a company. At least theoretically, if capital expenditures and repayment of loan principal can be postponed, if expenses can be held to a minimum, and if working capital need not be expanded, the entire amount of EBITDA can be handed over to investors as interest until the inevitable divestment takes place. No wonder investors are so fond of this measurement.

Although it does have its detractors in the investment community, I don't propose to address my problem with EBITDA from that perspective. My concern is the impact EBITDA has on the day-to-day management of businesses that are critical to both our personal and collective economic success. Because "what gets measured gets done" and so many of our businesses are now owned by private-equity firms who use EBIDTA as the key global performance measurement, I have found more and more managers of businesses who are also using EBITDA as guide in making both strategic and tactical business decisions. I have even encountered several who have gone so far as to use EBITDA as a measure of profit margin when quoting individual products. Having executives who base their day-to-day decisions on such a one-dimensional measure can prove to be a long-term disaster for any business and, possibly, our overall economic well-being.

The objective of a private-equity firm can be summed up as follows; buy a pig (or some pigs) with other peoples' money, spend a few years covering it with lipstick and starving it so it has a more elegant figure, and then sell the pig at a profit to someone who thinks it looks like Miss Universe. The key to the process is to be able to generate enough cash to pay for renting the "other peoples' money" while at the same time being able to afford all the lipstick. EBITDA turns out to be an effective measure for charting this process' success. There is nothing inherently evil in this process. The point is that the owners of a business managed in such a way appear to have no concern whatsoever for its long-term success or even its continued existence after it is sold. Their goal is to pay for the interest and lipstick until they can sell the pig at a profit.

With EBITDA as the measure emphasized by a company's owners, how can you blame the business' management (who serve at the owners' pleasure) from looking at each of their individual decisions in light of its impact on that measure? Just like teachers who "teach to the test" instead of teaching the fullness of their subject, top executives "manage to the measure" instead of managing for the long-term success of their organization (see Chapter Three). As a matter of fact, their position is not unlike that of the owners. Like soldiers in an ancient army, they have usually been brought in by the owners with the promise that they will share in the plunder at the end of the process so who can blame them for buying into the EBITDA measure. It is to their personal advantage when the process works.

Those who believe that the long-term growth of innovative and efficient businesses is critical to the economic success of our society should find this focus on the concept of EBITDA disturbing. It rewards short-sightedness and underachievement. It overlooks many of the factors that are critical to insuring the kinds of economically successful businesses that are fundamental to a well-functioning economy and society.

Let's explore just three of these factors; accrued liabilities, preserving the business' capital base, and employment of the company's assets.

Accrued Liabilities

One of the "tricks of the trade" is to accrue a big liability today to make it appear that profits have improved in the future when, in reality, the company would have been better off leaving things as they were.

For example, a company has a group of managers three years from retirement who collectively earn $5 million per year. Management makes these managers "an offer they can't refuse" to retire three years early at 60% of their normal pay and then replaces them with managers who will collectively earn $4 million annually. Upon the older managers' retirement, the company books a $9 million liability (60% of $5 million for three years) that will be paid off at $3 million per year.[1] The total cost of this commitment is expensed in the year the liability is booked.

In each of the next three years, $4 million is paid to the new managers and $3 million to the retirees. Although the cash paid for the work performed by these managers is now $7 million per year, the "expense" recorded on the books (and that is used to determine EBITDA) is only $4 million – a $1 million per year "savings" from the $5 million the company would have paid the former managers. At the end of three years, the company will have paid $21 million for the work performed by these positions instead of the $15 million it would have paid had the incumbents stayed in their jobs. Although EBITDA will have been $3 million higher, the company will be $6 million worse off – hardly a way to improve the organization's long-term performance.

Preserving the Business' Capital Base

In a note to Berkshire Hathaway's shareholders in 2000, Warren Buffett said, "References to EBITDA make us shudder." He indicated that the measure only makes sense, "if you think capital expenditures are funded by the tooth fairy."

A company needs to preserve its existing capital base if it is to stay in business (see Chapter Nine). The cost of funding this capital preservation process is a legitimate, ongoing business expense. Failure to incorporate this expense into the measurement of the company's performance overlooks a critical factor in determining its ability to simply survive over the long-term. Although depreciation expense as measured by GAAP-based accounting rules is an extremely poor way of measuring this cost, some measure must be included to determine whether or not the business is in the process of liquidating itself. By excluding depreciation and amortization (or some more relevant measure) from their key performance measure, owners and managers are showing their long-term disregard for the business and its other stakeholders.

Employment of the Company's Assets

EBITDA totally ignores the effective use of assets by management. It is not alone in doing so – the popular "profit as a percentage of sales" measure shares the same shortcoming (see Chapter Thirteen). To succeed in the long-term, a business must make good use of the funds it has tied up in its assets. Ignoring asset utilization encourages the use of outdated "batch and queue" concepts, the buildup of in-process and finished goods inventories, and sales to customers who take forever to pay their bills.

It is not only working capital that gets ignored. If a business has one productive asset worth $2 million it needs to earn twice the annual profit using that asset than it does when using another productive asset worth $1 million if both assets are to generate the same return on investment. Failure to incorporate some measure of the effectiveness of asset utilization excludes another critical factor in leading an organization toward a long-term successful future.

Is EBIDTA an Effective Measure for Private-Equity Firms?

In one of his insightful *DM Review* columns[2], Gary Cokins pointed out that a recent research study reported that less than half of the acquisitions studied reached their ROI goals.[3] Is it possible that potential buyers can actually distinguish between an emaciated pig coved with lipstick and the real Miss Universe? Is the short-term vision of the private-equity firm compounded by the short-term measure it uses to track its performance?

Perhaps it would even be better for the private-equity firm if they managed their investment with the objective of turning its underperforming investment into a powerful economic engine that will increase in real value for years and decades to come.

Conclusion

As discussed in Chapter One, the business world is populated with two types of executives: game players and stewards. Game players know how to play the game in a way that maximizes their personal gain with little or no regard for the damage they may inflict on the organizations they manage. Stewards don't look at their jobs as a game, but as a position in which they are entrusted with the task of insuring the long-term success of the organization they oversee and leaving it stronger when they depart than it was when they arrived. In our capitalist system, both are legitimate approaches to management. But the effect of playing games with our long-term ability to complete in the world economy cannot be positive.

Although EBITDA is one of many legitimate measures of a business' performance, emphasis on this one measurement – such as that made at many of today's highly-leveraged, short-term focused business – leads to long-term underachievement. As more and more organizations fall victim to this underachievement, its impact on the overall economy is inevitable.

As we move forward into an ever more competitive world marketplace, it is no wonder that we continue to lose ground. Using major companies in our key industries as a basis for playing games cannot bode well for the future and the growing focus on EBITDA as a measure of success only adds to the negative momentum we can already see all around us.

1 To keep the example simple while still making the point, the impact of discounting, taxes, etc. has been ignored.

2 http://www.dmreview.com/news/10001231-1.html

3 Deloitte Research – Economist Unit M&A Survey (2007)

Chapter Sixteen:
Don't Let Accountants Touch Cost Information –
It's the Law!

Ever since I read Robert Kaplan's article "Yesterday's Accounting Undermines Production" in the *Harvard Business Review* nearly a quarter century ago, I've spent my days (and many of my nights) assisting businesses of all types and sizes overcome the decision making problems caused by using traditional, out-of-date costing practices. In the process I've met and exchanged ideas with a myriad of academics, consultants, practitioners, and business executives from a wide variety of industries. I've also had the opportunity to share the knowledge I've gained through two books, scores of articles, dozens of executive letters and over one hundred presentations, seminars and webinars throughout North America. Based on feedback from these publications and events, the vast majority of those receiving the message have agreed that traditional costing methods are a serious problem that needs to be remedied if decision makers are to have the fact-based information they need to make quality decisions.

With such consistent positive feedback, it has always been puzzling to me why so few organizations have actually made a serious effort to correct the major deficiencies inherent in their methods of developing and presenting cost information to those executives that must make their organization's critical management decisions. The *2003 Best Accounting Practices* survey conducted by the Institute of Management Accountants and Ernst & Young added to this quandary when it reported that 98% of the surveyed financial executives believed that the cost information they provided to their management for decision making was inaccurate, but only about 20% planned on doing anything about it. My discussions with practitioners and executives since 2003 suggests that things have actually gotten worse, not better, since the survey.

Throughout my twenty-three years as a consultant, the most consistent obstacle I've encountered in convincing organizations to adopt more accurate and relevant costing practices has been the accountant – the trusted financial advisor of management who should be most concerned that the output of his or her labors has a positive effect on the organization's bottom line. In comparing notes with others in the business, I've found that accountants appear to be the universal obstacle to quality cost information.

In considering this issue over the years, I've explored many possible reasons. Are accountants just too lazy? Don't they understand how the cost information they provide can undermine their company's success? Is their influence so inconsequential that top management pays little or no attention to their suggestions? None of the answers to these questions has proven to be satisfactory. I can't believe that accountants are that lazy, don't care, or have so little influence. So why haven't they pressed the issue?

The conclusion I've come to is that accountants are simply not "wired" for costing. It's simply a matter of management putting the responsibility for decision costing information into the wrong hands. As a matter of fact, it's "the law" that causes the problem.

"The Law" and Cost Information[1]

The word "law" has two quite distinct meanings. It may describe *arbitrary regulations* made by human consent in particular circumstances for a particular purpose, and capable of being promulgated, enforced, suspended, altered, or rescinded without interference with the general scheme of the universe. On the other hand, the word "law" is also employed to designate *a generalized statement of observable fact*.

In the first sense we may talk of tax laws, the laws of civilized warfare, or the laws of baseball. Such laws frequently prescribe that certain events will follow upon certain others; but the second event is not a necessary consequence: the connection between the two is purely formal. For example, if a fielder catches a batted ball before it touches the ground, the batter is "out." There is, however, no inevitable connection between the capture of an in-flight baseball by a leather glove and the return of a human body from a patch of freshly mown lawn to a hard wooden bench. The two events are readily separable in theory. Should the rule-making body of baseball chose to alter the law, no cataclysm of nature would be involved.

Accountants are very adept at dealing with these types of laws. Their very existence is driven by laws; federal, state and local tax laws and regulations, FASB pronouncements, GAAP rules, SEC regulations, federal laws (like good old Sarbanes-Oxley), and many others. To keep abreast of these constantly changing laws and insure that their organizations comply with them while at the same time minimize the damage caused to its "bottom line," accountants must show exceptional intelligence and ingenuity.

In the second sense, we talk about the *laws of nature*. Such laws cannot be promulgated, altered, suspended, or broken at will; they are not laws at all in the sense that the laws of baseball or tax laws are laws. They are statements of observable facts inherent in the nature of the universe. Anybody can enact that murder will not be punishable by death; nobody can enact that the swallowing of a glass full of pure hydrocyanic acid shall not be punishable by death. In the former case, the connection between the two events is legal – that is, arbitrary; in the latter, it is a true causal connection. The second event is a necessary consequence of the first.

Unfortunately, accountants are not nearly as adept at dealing with these types of laws as they are at dealing with *arbitrary regulations*. Despite their intelligence and ingenuity, accountants view *laws of nature* against the background of the *arbitrary regulations* they have mastered. Their approach to internalizing these laws is to fit them into the context and constraints dictated by those *arbitrary regulations*. As a result, the way they view the economics of their organizations – and communicate that view to their management – seldom matches reality. The manner in which accountants handle cost information is a glaring example of this shortcoming.

Costs follow *laws of nature*, not *arbitrary regulations*. Costs do not care about GAAP, FASB pronouncements, tax rules, or SEC regulations. Costs are the result of actual cause-and-effect relationships. Operating a machine causes certain costs. Filling a customer's order causes certain costs. Moving and storing in-process inventory causes certain costs. Dealing with a high-maintenance customer causes costs. Outsourcing parts or processes not only reduces certain costs, it also causes new costs to be incurred. It doesn't matter what FASB says, what the SEC says, or what the IRS says, costs will react in a way dictated by *laws of nature*.

Accountants, Costs, and the Law

Putting the development and maintenance of cost information into the hands of accountants is like putting the development of a new snack food into the hands of chocoholics. Just as it is inevitable that the new snack food will be some form of chocolate regardless of what new product the market wants or what products the plant is good at manufacturing, it is inevitable that the main focus of any cost information developed by accountants will be focused on complying with the *arbitrary regulations* that are their raison d'être. Costs will not reflect reality; instead they will reflect years of compromise by countless committees influenced by endless interest groups and government agencies.

How many accountants have created cost information systems that do not tie into or support the general ledger? There are very few indeed. This observation alone should highlight the accountant's agenda when put in charge of cost information; namely, the cost system exists to support the financial accounting system. If that is all a cost system is intended to do, a company might just as well save the money and go back to the "pickle barrel" system (count how may pickles are in the barrel when you start, add the number of pickles you bought, subtract the pickles in the barrel when you finish and the difference must be the number of pickles you sold).

Consider the cost information at a typical manufacturer. The cost accounting system only includes "inventoriable" costs – those costs the promulgators of *arbitrary regulations* consent to have treated as an asset in the manufacturer's general ledger. Further, it is only required that the method of applying these costs to the individual items in the manufacturer's inventory result in a reasonably accurate valuation of the manufacturer's inventory *as a whole*. It is not necessary for any individual item to be valued accurately as long as it all averages out when applied to entire organization. It is not necessary for any manufacturing process to be measured appropriately. It is not necessary for any non-manufacturing costs to be measured and it is forbidden that such costs be included. The cost system focus is on value in inventory not cost to the organization — two totally different objectives — and it ignores non-manufacturing costs altogether.

Since the *arbitrary regulations* which guide the accountant are so focused on value in inventory, anything that seems superfluous to attaining that goal is generally cast aside as being unnecessary. The result is minimalist, "short-cut" costing. It is costing that Mo Bayou at the University of Michigan – Dearborn describes as "going around a company's processes, not through them." If all you need is an accurate value of total inventory, why do more work than is necessary to meet that objective? The accountant sees no cost / benefit in measuring the cost of manufacturing processes, definitely sees none in measuring the cost of non-manufacturing processes, and doesn't see why costing that goes around a company's processes does not provide good enough numbers to apply to individual products and services.

As suggested earlier, paying attention to the *laws of nature* — not just *arbitrary regulations* — clearly identifies costing issues that the typical accountant will totally overlook. How about including a cost of capital to understand the economic impact of carrying raw, in-process and finished inventory? How about looking through the windshield and incorporating the cost of preserving the company's capital asset base instead of simply looking in the rear-view mirror and writing off the irrelevant sunk costs of past capital acquisitions? How about post-manufacturing activities? Is there no cost related to storing finished goods prior to shipment? Are order processing, picking, assembly, packing and shipment activities all free? How about the different levels of effort required to acquire, handle and store the company's variety of raw materials and purchased goods? How about the costs required to support offshore vendors or the outside contractors to whom the company has outsourced former in-house manufacturing processes? How about the disproportional amount of work that goes into managing the company's biggest "jerk" customer?

Accountants have too many other things to do — most of them legally required as the result of *arbitrary regulations* — to pay much attention to the decision support needs of management. Even when they do address those needs, however, they make sure they comply in ways that help solve accounting's problems first and foremost.

If Not Accountants, Then Who?

In nearly a quarter century of working the field of cost measurement and management, I have found that those most effective at developing and maintaining effective cost systems are individuals with backgrounds in mathematics or engineering. Individuals with accounting backgrounds rank near the bottom, just ahead of those from sales.

I believe those with math and engineering backgrounds are effective in the field of costing because effective costing is driven by a quest for "the truth" and both mathematics and engineering are disciplines that attempt to understand "the truth." Mathematicians are trained to replicate the *laws of nature* in terms of mathematics and are not afraid to tackle relationships slightly more complex than $a \times b = c$. Engineers – particularly industrial engineers and their derivative specialties – must understand the *laws of nature* if they are to develop solutions to problems that are constrained by and must comply with them. This has become especially true during the past few decades as industrial engineers have cast off the image of stop-watch-wielding efficiency police and become innovative problem solvers who regularly apply principles that would have been considered heresy just two decades ago.

Accountants rank low because they are allowed – and are often required – to ignore *laws of nature* and simply comply with *arbitrary regulations*. Their obsession with "the rules" and reporting history have blinded them to the responsibility they bear in providing management with accurate and relevant cost information on which to base its decisions. Although their work is critical to a business' success, sales professionals have shown themselves to be the "court jesters" of costing. They've become preconditioned to disbelieve uncomfortable truths that might make a sale difficult while firmly believing favorable untruths based on very shaky rationale that might make a sale easier. Their view of logic changes to fit their desired results.

As I reflect on the hundreds of individuals I have worked with during the past twenty-three years – both as clients and as consulting partners – I cannot think of a single individual with a mathematics background who did not prove to be extremely competent at developing, maintaining, and using cost information. I would rank three-quarters of the engineers I've worked with in the same category. Accountants often start out strong, but within a short period of time all but about one-quarter regress back to their "blue blankets" by returning their focus to compliance with *arbitrary regulations* at the expense of the *laws of nature*. Finally, although we cannot live without good sales professionals, I can remember very few who took cost information seriously. To them it was all a game. They believed what was convenient for them to believe and disbelieved what was convenient for them to disbelieve.

The Solution – Don't Let Accountants Touch Cost Information

The solution is to recognize that cost accounting and cost information are not the same thing. Cost accounting supports financial accounting systems. Cost information supports decision making systems. The only thing the two have in common is the word "cost." One reports history for outsiders while the other projects future possible outcomes for insiders. One is driven by *arbitrary regulations* while the other is driven by *laws of nature*. The knowledge, experience and mindset necessary to master the two disciplines are vastly different.

As a consequence, those individuals responsible for decision costing should be separated from those responsible for cost accounting and placed under the direction of a non-financial executive. Those responsible for cost information that supports decision making should understand the business thoroughly, have top-notch problem solving and modeling skills, be skilled at decision economics, and understand how to convert the laws of nature into simple mathematical algorithms. Decision costing is not brain surgery; it is the application of common sense to real life situations – common sense that should not be constrained by the *arbitrary regulations* that form the lens through which accountants view all business activity.

I understand that this solution is not original; that responsibility for developing cost information to support management decisions lies outside of finance and accounting in many European and Asian companies. Companies in those parts of the world mastered total quality and lean thinking before North American companies took notice, maybe they're right about the organizational positioning of those who develop and maintain decision costing information as well.

Conclusion

It is inadvisable to place the development and maintenance of cost information that is intended to support critical decisions made by a company's management in the hands of accountants. Accountants are experts on the *arbitrary regulations* created by human beings to regulate and control society. Organizations cannot function in a complex society without the intelligence and ingenuity of a group of competent accountants. This does not, however, make accountants experts on everything. A typical accountant's education and experience has little or nothing to do with understanding *laws of nature* and translating those laws into truthful, insightful, and understandable tools that will help their company's decision makers make good decisions and take effective actions.

Individuals with mathematics or engineering backgrounds, on the other hand, have spent their entire careers trying to create valid models of reality – models that reflect *laws of nature*. Prior to the Securities and Exchange Acts in the early 1930s – *arbitrary regulations* that changed the focus of cost information – these were the primary types of individuals employed to measure and manage costs. From Josiah Wedgwood to Alexander Hamilton Church, the pioneers of costing were not accountants. Maybe now is the time to begin obeying the *laws of nature* again and move the responsibility for developing and maintaining cost information away from *arbitrary regulation*-oriented accountants to the mathematicians and engineers who understand that business must operate in a world of reality.

---

[1] The discussion of "laws" in this article is based on Chapter One, "The 'Laws' of Nature and Opinion," from Dorothy L. Sayers classic 1941 book, *The Mind of the Maker*.

About the author...
DOUGLAS T. HICKS, CPA, CMC

Douglas T. Hicks, CPA, CMC is President of D. T. Hicks & Co., a consulting firm concentrating on the decision costing needs of small and mid-sized organizations. Before establishing his firm in 1985, he accumulated over fifteen years of financial and management accounting experience, twelve of those years in industry. A graduate of the University of Michigan – Dearborn's School of Management, he is a member of the Michigan Association of CPAs, the Institute of Management Accountants and the Institute of Management Consultants. In 1997, he received the University of Michigan - Dearborn Alumni Association's *Professional Growth and Scholarship Award* for his work in advancing modern costing concepts.

Since 1985, Doug has worked with over two hundred businesses to develop cost-effective methods for developing the accurate and relevant cost information they need to lead them into a more profitable future. This work has resulted in *the "abc" solution*™, an "activity-based" decision support process that enables businesses to develop the accurate and relevant cost information they need to make effective pricing, product/service line management, customer relationship, capital investment, cost reduction, and other critical decisions **without investing in specialized software or implementing a new cost accounting system**. His client organizations range from $2 million to over $3 billion in annual sales and have included firms in health care, packaging, distribution, printing, and marketing services as well as automotive, aerospace, food, furniture, heavy duty equipment, and other manufacturers.

As Doug's approach has become more widely known and accepted as a cost-effective approach for adopting "activity-based" concepts, he has become a frequent speaker on the subject. Trade and professional associations regularly use him as a resource for their members. The popularity of Doug's down-to-earth approach to management accounting topics has made him a regular speaker for the Institute of Management Accountants. In addition to including his one-day seminar in their nationwide REAP Program, he was a featured speaker at the IMA's 1993, 1994, 1996, 1998 and 2007 national conferences and in 2005 he served as chairman and lead speaker for their national conference's *Cost and Performance Measurement and Maturity* track. In 1998, he was selected the IMA's *Instructor of the Year*, an award based on the results of course evaluations turned in by conference and seminar participants.

Doug's articles have been published in a wide variety of professional and trade magazines including *Journal of Accountancy*, *Cost Management*, *ActionLine*, *Plastic Technology*, *Modern Casting*, *Precision*, *Printing Manager*, *Manufacturing Engineering*, *Leadership Excellence*, and *Management Accounting*. His two books, *Activity-Based Costing for Small and Mid-Sized Businesses: An Implementation Guide (1992)* and *Activity-Based Costing: Making it Work for Small and Mid-Sized Companies (1998)*, both published by John Wiley & Sons, have sold over 15,000 copies worldwide. He has also written several industry specific guides for adopting activity-based concepts and contributed chapters to others' works on management accounting and supply chain management.

You can learn more and contact Doug through D. T. Hicks & Co.'s website at www.dthicksco.com.

CMC (Certified Management Consultant) is a certification mark awarded by the Institute of Management Consultants USA and represents evidence of the highest standards of consulting and adherence to the ethical canons of the profession. Less than 1% of all consultants have achieved this level of performance.

Made in the USA
Monee, IL
18 February 2021

60800161R00069